THE
ILLUMINATION
PROCESS

Also by Alberto Villoldo, Ph.D.

COURAGEOUS DREAMING:
*How Shamans Dream the World into Being**

YOGA, POWER, & SPIRIT:
*Pantanjali the Shaman**

THE FOUR INSIGHTS: Wisdom, Power,
*and Grace of the Earthkeepers**

MENDING THE PAST AND HEALING

*THE FUTURE WITH SOUL RETRIEVAL**

SHAMAN, HEALER, SAGE:
How to Heal Yourself and Others with the
Energy Medicine of the Americas

ONE SPIRIT MEDICINE:
Ancient Ways to Ultimate Wellness

DANCE OF THE FOUR WINDS:
Secrets of the Inca Medicine Wheel

ISLAND OF THE SUN:
Mastering the Inca Medicine Wheel

*Available from Hay House

Please visit Hay House USA: www.hayhouse.com®
Hay House Australia: www.hayhouse.com.au
Hay House UK: www.hayhouse.co.uk
Hay House India: www.hayhouse.co.in

THE ILLUMINATION PROCESS

A Shamanic Guide to Transforming Toxic Emotions into Wisdom, Power, and Grace

Alberto Villoldo

HAY HOUSE, INC.
Carlsbad, California • New York City
London • Sydney • New Delhi

Published in the United States by: Hay House, Inc.: www.hayhouse.com
Published in Australia by: Hay House Australia Pty. Ltd.: www.hayhouse.com.au
Published in the United Kingdom by: Hay House UK, Ltd.: www.hayhouse.co.uk
Published in India by: Hay House Publishers India: www.hayhouse.co.in

Interior layout: Bryn Starr Best

Originally published as *Illumination* 978-1401923280.

Library of Congress Control Number: 2017942144

ISBN: 978-1-4019-5354-6

11 10 9 8 7 6 5 4 3

1st edition, March 2010
2nd edition, March 2011
3rd edition, July 2017

Certified Chain of Custody
Promoting Sustainable Forestry
www.sfiprogram.org
SFI-01268

SFI label applies to the text stock

Printed in the United States of America

To Marcela Lobos.
You showed me the way.

CONTENTS

Preface: *A Taste of Infinity*   ix

Chapter 1:   Initiation as Illumination   1

Chapter 2:   The Hunter and the Hunted   25

Chapter 3:   Taming the Prehistoric Brain   43

Chapter 4:   Archetypal Death and the Great Awakening   61

Chapter 5:   The Stages of Initiation   83

Chapter 6:   Seven Demons and Seven Angels   101

Chapter 7:   Vanquishing the Demons of Youth   111

Chapter 8:   Vanquishing the Demons of Maturity   125

Chapter 9:   The Initiations of Youth   143

Chapter 10: The Initiations of Maturity   157

Chapter 11: The Shaman's Gifts: Building Personal Power   175

Conclusion   183

Endnotes   191

Acknowledgments   193

About the Author   195

PREFACE

A Taste of Infinity

I have spent many years in the Andes Mountains and in the Amazon Rainforest studying the indigenous wisdom keepers and documenting their healing practices. Although these men and women are also shamans, I will use the more traditional name of Laika to refer to these wisdom keepers, to differentiate them from the ordinary herbalists, midwives, and healers. Initially, I sought to understand how their spiritual medicine could help alleviate the host of ailments that humanity suffers from today. It took me many years to understand that shamans don't subscribe to the model of illness that we hold in the West. For them, all disease has spiritual origins, and illness is manifested through subtle bodies—the energy body, our emotions, our thoughts—and lastly the physical body. For the shamans, physical and emotional challenges provide an opportunity for initiation and spiritual rebirth into a new way of being. If the opportunity for initiation is missed, a second wake-up call might come in the form of an even more serious malady.

In this book you will discover that the most powerful way to successfully face physical and emotional problems is to undergo a sacred initiation that leads to the death of your old self, to rebirth, and to your illumination. The illumination is not a distant achievement attained after years of sitting on a meditation cushion, or something that strikes suddenly. Most shamans dismiss these as religious flights of the imagination, or a postponement to a distant future what is readily available today. Nor is illumination merely an understanding of the nature of good and evil, and how in a metaphysical sense neither exists. For the shamans it is a series of awakenings and realizations that we pass through again and again. These illuminations are a part of our developmental journey, and we don't discard any of them as we ascend to the higher rungs. We transcend and include them and grow beyond our earlier levels of understanding while including each illumination as part of an integrated self.

Illumination helps you attain an exalted understanding of your life journey; it brings you freedom from emotional suffering and an awareness of the true nature of reality. Along the way, emotional and physical healing can take place, and, like many great shamans, you may develop the power to heal others, to read the signs of destiny in nature, and to face death fearlessly. For the shaman, illumination is not an internal state of awareness only. You must bring your gifts forth into the world in the form of compassion, courage, and humility, which are rare attributes to come by these days. Illumination has been called by many names in post-shamanic societies—*samadhi*, bliss, enlightenment, and it is distinctly like the Christian concept of grace. Many religions teach that grace can only be bestowed by God, as happened to Saint Paul when he had his conversion experience on the road to Damascus, or to the Prophet Muhammad when he received the Qur'an from the angel Gabriel. Traditionally, we've believed that grace cannot be gained by our own individual efforts. But is it true?

The Laika intuited what researchers in neuroscience are discovering today: illumination is an inherent faculty of the brain, and not just a gift that some higher power bestows upon us. And while indeed it was possible to receive truth and knowledge directly from Spirit through mysterious means, they discovered that they could attain illumination by successfully completing certain initiations into the mysteries of life. There are seven life passages we all experience during our lives—birth, manhood or womanhood, first love, marriage, parenthood, sagehood, and death. To experience these as initiations requires us to face and defeat our inner demons, comprehend our oneness with Creation, and understand our duty as the stewards of all life.

Anything short of illumination is not a complete healing. Shamanic healers don't distinguish cancer, diabetes, or heart disease in their cosmology. They see these conditions and many others as symptoms of a spiritual illness—the loss of a sacred sense of oneness with the universe, and our neglecting our role as participants in Creation. To a Laika there is no difference between being killed by a jaguar and being killed by a microbe. To Westerners, being killed by a microbe is an illness, whereas being eaten by a jaguar is an accident, pure bad luck. A Laika knows that he has to be in sacred relationship with jaguars and microbes alike, or else both are going to look at him as dinner. In addition, the Laika knows that he must take part in dreaming the world into being as a participant in creation, or else continue repeating the nightmare of history and have to settle for a world that is being dreamed by others.

Religions have portrayed illumination as something nearly impossible for ordinary humans to attain. The Laika believe that illumination is possible for all who are willing to embark courageously on their journey of initiation. The maps for navigating this territory have been drawn by the great masters, including Christ and Buddha, but we must be willing to follow the path of initiation ourselves, as all great teachers have done. When we do so, we become explorers and pioneers. We break free from the genetic and psychological legacies that we inherited— traits that predispose us to live and die in certain ways. Only then can we begin to craft truly healthy, authentic, and original lives. We are able to grow new bodies that age and heal and die gracefully. We are illumined.

Are our brains programmed for enlightenment? The evolutionary journey from matter to mind to soul to spirit—each step of which transcends and includes the step below it—makes me think that illumination might be an inherent guiding force of nature. First it's the lone individual reaching for the heavens and touching infinity, then more and more of us follow, until all of humanity discovers our transcendent nature.

Perhaps this is the stuff of daydreams. My scientific education taught me that matter sprang out of nothing during the Big Bang, and that life is making its way darkly and soundlessly to a cold death at the end of time. For many years I believed the explanation of scientific materialism to be the only true one. But after my own initiation, and after having tasted infinity, I discovered I prefer the company of visionaries, of men and women who know that their destiny is to dream the world into being. I hope you'll join us!

Alberto Villoldo, Ph.D.
www.thefourwinds.com

CHAPTER 1

Initiation as Illumination

Third week in the Amazon. Everything is moist. I've put away my favorite fountain pen and started writing with a pencil. I tried reading yesterday's entry, but it was a smear of blue on the page.

The sun is breaking through the canopy, and the dewdrops on the spiderweb before me sparkle like jewels. Nature is teaching me this morning how death is essential for life, providing it nourishment. There is a spider in the Amazon that spins a silken cocoon around its prey as the creature struggles in vain to break free. This morning it has captured a moth, and the spider is darting back and forth, weaving, binding its victim, like the Lilliputians hurriedly trapping Gulliver with their tiny ropes. Once the creature is firmly tied, the spider injects it with a venom that breaks down all its tissues and liquefies its insides, and then it proceeds to suck the life from its catch. The spider has several such "meals" stored in its web. Whenever it requires food, it pierces the shell of its prey with a needle-like feeder and snacks on the fermenting proteins inside. After it has feasted, all that's left are empty husks that were once blue-winged moths and yellow bumblebees.

"The spider is the only one that does not get caught in the web," said don Antonio.

I looked up into the eyes of the old Indian who was my guide and mentor.

"That is the world you live in, my friend, a world of predators and prey, where people suck one another dry. There is another world, the world of creators, that you know nothing about."

I live in the world of predators? Or is it the world of prey, in which I am captured, consumed, powerless?

Don Antonio knew that I felt I was in an exhausting battle with life and hoped to find answers here in the Amazon.

"You want to escape for a while, and then return to your world and conquer your enemies," he said. "But you must conquer them here, because they are inside of you."

Journal
Marañon River, Peru

There are seven great initiations every human being must undergo. They are the initiations of birth, manhood or womanhood, first love, marriage (and sometimes divorce), parenthood, sagehood, and death. It's possible that you won't go through all of these passages in a biological sense or at the usual time of life. For example, some people never marry or have children. Yet each of us, regardless of gender or culture, must go through them *mythically* at least once. If you have no son or daughter, you may write a book or produce some other creative project that will be your "baby," which you must learn how to parent. You will be "born" again as you start a new life in another city or change careers, and parts of you will "die" metaphorically with the losses and changes that life brings. Initiations are inevitable. If you resist initiation, the universe will conspire to bring you face to face with the end of a stage of your life in some other way. Resistance is futile.

Every initiation presents you with the opportunity for illumination—to awaken your divine nature, identify with the realm of the creators, experience grace, and break free of the realm of scarcity and the brutish, predatory existence that most of humanity endures. If you miss one of your initiations, your health and emotional well-being will be compromised. For example, if you don't complete the initiation of marriage, you may not be able to achieve true intimacy with a partner after the romance wears off. If you miss your initiation into manhood, you may become a *puer aeternus*, an eternal boy, collecting "toys" your entire life. Psychology tells us that to fix these situations, we must understand what traumas we suffered as children, or how our dysfunctional parents taught us unhealthy behaviors. But dissecting the past is a trap. The shaman knows that focusing on our wounds will only reinforce them as we begin to believe that the dramatic personal stories—tragic or heroic—that we tell ourselves about our past are who we are today.

You can only heal fully when you successfully complete the initiations presented to you by life. In later chapters you will be able to identify the initiations you might have missed, prepare to face them courageously, and next time the wheel of fortune lands on your name, be ready to respond to their hidden calling.

Our Unhealed Emotions

Initiation offers us the opportunity to heal our emotions. All the drama and suffering in our lives is brought about by our unhealed emotions, which give rise to our beliefs about how the world works. The shaman understands that whatever beliefs you hold about the nature of reality, the universe will prove you right. If you venture into the woods for an evening walk with an uneasy feeling, you will hear the branches snapping ominously nearby. If you believe that every relationship you enter into will end in disaster, it probably will. If you're convinced that you will never succeed at work, you won't. Conversely, positive beliefs help you to see the glass as always half full. If you believe you deserve to be happy, happiness will find you even in trying circumstances. If you believe the woods are safe and beautiful, they will be so.

Our unhealed emotions are the source of our deeply ingrained beliefs that convince us that a particular situation is a problem we are powerless to change. We can solve any difficulty in our lives— from discovering love to achieving peace in our world—if we heal our emotions and then change our beliefs. But we cannot simply change our minds and magically make the world be different, because our beliefs are etched into neural networks deep inside our brain. These beliefs are encrypted as emotion-laden programs that evolved during prehistoric times for dealing with survival, violence, and fear. Reprogramming these neural networks is not as simple as talking about them to a therapist. Thinking positive thoughts is a start, but you can't change your beliefs about love or abundance just by putting a new affirmation on your refrigerator door. You must rewire your brain.

The Seven Passages

Every culture on the planet recognizes the seven passages or initiations that human beings have undergone since the dawn of time. Each initiation marks a break with the past that invites you to step into who you are becoming, and thus attain illumination.

These initiations can be experienced as only hormonal and physiological changes that accompany each passage, or they can be lived mythically, with full attention to the emotional and intellectual landscapes that they open up. A mythic initiation requires the death of a personal story and an archetypal rebirth into a new and greater personal myth.[1] Carl Jung is credited with developing this concept in the context of the psychology of the unconscious. The archetypes manifest in symbolism, or imagery in dreams and fantasies, art and literature, mythology and religion. They may be personified characters such as the Great Mother, or the Wise Old Man; or processes such as death, rebirth, and the marriage of opposites. With each passage you discover that you do not die, even when you think the heartbreak is going to kill you, or the loss of your youth is going to devastate you. Eventually, your initiation leads to the discovery of peace, generosity, compassion, and illumination.

If you're able to recognize when you're on the threshold and bravely surrender to the process of initiation, you'll come through the pain and stop feeling that life is something that happens to you. When you experience your initiation, your feelings of powerlessness and fear dissipate, and in their place arise courage, curiosity, and creativity. You can finally break the spell that caused you to be drained by all the dramatic events of your past.

There are seven toxic emotions that must be confronted during initiation and that give rise to every limiting belief we hold. For some strange reason, nature programmed these emotions into the human brain. They were once known as the seven deadly sins, and even personified as demons, because of their extraordinary power.

- Wrath
- Envy
- Greed
- Gluttony
- Lust
- Pride
- Sloth

When we break free from these deadly emotions and the beliefs they create about scarcity, powerlessness, intimacy, and fear, we discover that although there is violence in the world, we can live free of violence in our home and in our relationships. We learn that although greed and gluttony are rampant, we can live in abundance without developing obese bodies or avaricious lifestyles. We discover that although it is very difficult to change the world, it is not difficult to change our own world.

Initiation is how shamans heal toxic emotions and transform them into fountains of power and grace. A rite of initiation makes it possible for you to grow without getting mired in adversity and suffering. It allows you to heal through your own power, instead of recruiting others to be bit players in your emotional dramas. I once heard a wise old man say that if you do not discover the lessons that toxic emotions have to teach you, you'll end up marrying someone who will make sure you learn them. Until we heal these deadly emotions, we will continue attracting people who share the same emotional wounds and stories we play out. Opposites may attract in the world of physics, but in human relationships fear breeds terror, and generosity attracts plenitude.

Initiation brings even greater blessings than the healing of negative emotions. It leads us to illumination, which allows us to know our divine nature and to encounter Spirit in action, in the great playground of Creation. At last we have escaped the web of predators and prey, and entered the world of creators—a unified world where we are both the canvas and the artist, the landscape and the paintbrush.

Although all cultures have elaborate rites of passage for young men and women, these are seldom profound initiations. Birth is too often merely an occasion for a social ceremony or a homemade video, while death is something to avoid confronting at all costs. Similarly, the deep union of two souls is not achieved by an elaborate wedding party; the entry into manhood is not accomplished by shooting an animal, nor is womanhood achieved by getting a menstrual period; and conceiving a child does not make you a parent. No single event can prepare you for the challenges you will face in a significant new stage of life. True initiation is a response to an inner calling; it requires that you face personal challenges heroically and experience a genuine rebirth into a new way of being.

Initiations often force you to defy convention, as in the historical love affair between the Roman general Mark Antony and Cleopatra, the Queen of Egypt—a relationship that brought embarrassment to the Roman Empire and inspiration to many lovers as in Shakespeare's dramatization of it in the tragedy *Antony and Cleopatra*. Like Mark Antony, even ordinary people sometimes risk everything they once valued to follow love, succeed in a career, or be good parents. Initiation is an invitation to discover the real significance of existence and play the game of life at a new and higher level.

Once your initiation is under way, your toxic emotions will heal as you transform them into the seven virtues, known as "angels" during the Middle Ages:

- Peace
- Generosity
- Purity of intent
- Courage
- Compassion
- Temperance
- Humility

Traditional Initiation	Emotional Experience If You Fail Your Initiation	Demons and Angels
Birth	You struggle with belonging, self-worth, and anger. You feel as if you don't belong in this world.	Wrath, healed by Peace
Manhood or Womanhood	You're narcissistic, resentful about what you lack, and obsessed with materialism and power.	Greed, healed by Generosity
First Love	You search in vain for the perfect partner, feeling lonely and incomplete. You are unable to have a sexual experience in which you surrender to intimacy.	Lust, healed by Purity of Intent
Marriage	You're the eternal single, ambivalent about relationships. You expect your partner to meet all your needs and are unwilling to work at creating a genuine partnership.	Sloth, healed by Courage
Parenthood	You live through your child or your projects, obsessing about outcomes. You're envious of those who seem to have more options—and even of your own child's wide-open vistas.	Envy, healed by Compassion
Sagehood	You are crippled by a sense of scarcity and loss, and the desire to regain what is no more. You consume more than you need in order to feel better about yourself.	Gluttony, healed by Temperance
The Great Crossing	You cling to unfinished business. You become arrogant and self-important, and terrified of your own mortality.	Pride, healed by Humility

Life invites us to be initiated through many means: through the possibility of love, the death of a parent or friend, the birth of a child, or a serious health crisis. When we succeed in our initiation, we become illumined with the light of wisdom and understanding. We are able to perceive reality as it truly is, unclouded by our emotional wounds and hurts. But when we refuse the call to initiation, we become caught like a moth in the spiderweb, struggling to escape a predicament filled with pain and drama. Wouldn't it be better to enter the landscape of inevitable change willingly and gracefully? If we succeed, initiation can be the doorway through which we step onto a path that leads to a life of passion, authenticity, and grace. But it requires that we say yes again and again to our initiations and boldly explore unknown territory.

Jonah's Initiation

One of my favorite tales of initiation is the biblical story of Jonah, who is called by God to go to Nineveh and teach the people there. Jonah is comfortable at home raising his children and dealing with everyday domestic affairs. When he hears God's call, his response is to run as fast as he can in the opposite direction. Jonah is not interested in heeding this calling; in fact, he's horrified by the thought that he could be more than a simple fisherman. He believes he doesn't have it in him to be a messenger of hope and doubts that he could ever amount to anything more than a simple man who guts fish every morning. Terrified that he might fail at the task he has been given, Jonah boards a ship to get as far away as he can from his calling. When the vessel encounters heavy storms in the Mediterranean, the sailors suspect that someone has defied God, and they toss Jonah into the sea, where he is promptly swallowed by a whale. He remains in the whale's belly until he is finally spat out—on the shores of Nineveh.

The moral of the story is that life will drag us kicking and screaming to our destiny if we try to escape it. Our choice is to be delivered in grace and beauty, which happens when we say yes to our initiation, or covered in whale spit, which happens when we reject it. The whale in the story represents our emotions, a huge and irresistible power that threatens to swallow us and keep us trapped for days or years. Remember how long you were stuck in a painful relationship, angry with yourself and your partner, long after you realized it was time to leave? We can spend many years in the belly of the whale dealing with our rage; or our sense of not having the right partner or the right life; or our envy for the youth, success, or wealth others have that we might lack. Eventually the whale spits us out at the shores we were meant to reach. When Jonah arrives on the shores at Nineveh, he is ready to follow his calling, unhesitant and fully able to access his power and to understand his mission. The shaman understands that there are more elegant ways to get to Nineveh than in the belly of a whale.

During my travels in the Amazon as an anthropologist, I witnessed many rituals that initiated young men into manhood and young women into marriage or motherhood. But these, like our own Western ceremonies, were often choreographed festivities disconnected from their deeper meaning. Initiation, by contrast, is nothing less than an invitation to an unimaginable destiny. It is fraught with danger and opportunity. The outcome is not guaranteed. It requires a courageous response, and invites us to become the hero of our own journey. Initiation can take place within the secret confines of your heart, where you go to meet the Divine within, or in the exterior realm, anywhere in the world. Regardless of whether it is an inner or an outer journey, if you're successful you will be blessed and graced. If you fail, you may live to regret it, and die the slow death of an empty and hollow life.

The Four Steps of the Buddha's Journey

When we succeed in our initiation, we attain illumination. For Buddhists, illumination is a state free from suffering and rebirth known as *bodhi*, literally "awakening." In one school of Buddhism, the ideal is to become a *bodhisattva*, a man or woman dedicated to the awakening of all living beings.

The Buddha, who had lived a sheltered life of luxury as the young prince Siddhartha, was called to his initiation at the age of 29 when he first left the palace and traveled into the countryside. Along the way he saw a bent old man, and asked his charioteer if age would befall all people. When his driver said yes, the prince was disturbed. As he continued, he witnessed disease, hunger, and death in the form of a rotting corpse. Siddhartha was confused and distraught, for the "ugly" side of life had been kept from him during his youth. Now his innocence was shattered by the reality outside the palace walls, and no doubt he realized that he too would share the same fate as his subjects. In what is known as the Buddha's "great departure," the young prince renounced his life of ease, shaved his head like a monk, and went into the streets to beg for his food. The great departure represents an essential element of every initiation—leaving behind the comfort of the familiar, a difficult renunciation even when the familiar is painful, as in a bad job or relationship.

The Buddha could not have attained his illumination sipping tea in the palace gardens. He had to step into the unknown world outside the palace. The king sent servants to entice the prince with food and drink, but the young Buddha-to-be refused to return home. He did not allow himself to be seduced by his previous life. Instead, he sat in silence under a fig tree and turned his attention inward in meditation until he found the answers he sought: Why must we suffer? Is there any way out? Imagine sitting under the shade of a tree in the blistering Indian heat—not an easy task, with flies landing on your face, attractive young women strolling by, lepers sleeping next to you, and children shouting and playing around you, not to mention the gnawing hunger in your gut. Siddhartha confronted all of these challenges internally. He must have faced every fear and every demon conceivable to man.

In the end, the Buddha discovered that suffering could be eliminated altogether. After his illumination, he returned with a gift of wisdom that he shared with all who would listen. The Four Noble Truths remain at the core of Buddhism today. They are:

- Life is suffering: birth is suffering; aging is suffering; illness is suffering; death is suffering; sorrow, grief, and despair are suffering.

- Suffering is caused by craving and desire.

- By giving up craving and desire, you attain freedom from suffering.

- This path is achieved through right view, right intention, right speech, right action, right livelihood, right effort, right mindfulness, and right concentration.

The teachings of Buddhism have spread all over the world, for the Four Noble Truths are a universal wisdom. But just as important is the Buddha's journey of initiation—a call to action that each of us must embark on, for by doing so we will learn to overcome suffering in our own lives. Should we remain content just hearing about the Buddha's teaching, instead of going ourselves to meditate under a tree? Is it enough to just read about the 40 days that Jesus spent in the desert, instead of going out on our own vision quest? My answer is that we must find out for ourselves what the masters and sages discovered, in order to attain our own illumination. We will accomplish this by embarking on the journey of initiation.

The Buddha's illumination perfectly illustrates the four stages of the journey of initiation:

1. The awakening: recognizing your dilemma ("There is death and disease, and I am trapped inside a palace.")

2. The great departure: embarking on your journey ("I am a monk and shave my head.")

3. The tests: confronting challenges and adversity ("I sit in stillness.")

4. Illumination: the return to bring gifts of knowledge to others ("We can all be free from suffering.")

We will return to these stages in Chapter 4 for a continued discussion.

Psyche's Initiation

The myth of Eros and Psyche can be seen as a feminine journey of initiation. Psyche was the most beautiful daughter of a powerful king. While her sisters had no trouble finding husbands, Psyche's beauty was intimidating and no man dared approach her for her hand in marriage. In fact, her beauty was so great that she began to be worshipped as the mortal incarnation of Aphrodite—the goddess of beauty. This misperception angered Aphrodite, so she sent her son Eros (also known as Cupid) to strike Psyche with one of his enchanted arrows and make her fall irreversibly in love with a hideous monster. Eros took to the task with great passion, but in the end fell madly in love with Psyche. He brought Psyche into a beautiful palace, made her his bride, and granted her every wish, with the one condition that she never look at his face in the light. Thus he visited her only at night, when they shared their company and their passion.

Psyche had every material possession her heart desired, and she was happy for some time. However, she eventually became dissatisfied with her life. During the day, when Eros wasn't around, she was lonely. She missed her family and her friends. Feeling pity for her sadness, Eros brought Psyche's sisters to the palace to visit. In her dissatisfied state, Psyche was convinced by her evil sisters that she had married a monster, and she became determined to know her husband for all that he was. One night, while Eros was sleeping, Psyche held a lamp to her husband's face to see his true identity, and she was stunned to find the beautiful god of love. In her amazement, a drop of hot oil fell from the lamp, scalding Eros's shoulder and waking him, at which point he fled, leaving her devastated.

Psyche's story illustrates the importance of the first stage of initiation, the awakening—the recognition of your dilemma and how it confines you. Siddhartha was compelled to witness real life outside the palace. Psyche was compelled to see her husband's real face—to no longer be simply a nighttime bride. Psyche's awakening is the first call to initiation.

Psyche's great departure was the revealing of her husband's true self. She steps away from what she has known—the beautiful palace, the material comforts, the agreement that has kept her in the dark—and begins her journey. This is a journey of true and fulfilling love.

The journey continues with the third step of initiation: the tests. Psyche goes to Aphrodite's temple and requests the return of her beloved. The goddess agrees, but only if Psyche completes four tasks that Aphrodite knows are nearly impossible. Yet Psyche gladly takes them on, despite being aware that she could easily lose her life in any of these endeavors. She begins her mission, which includes a dangerous journey to the underworld, where she faces Cerberus, the many-headed dog who guards the gates of Hades, the realm of death.

As Psyche is returning from her final task—the retrieval of a beauty potion from the underworld—she falls into a death-like sleep, representing the symbolic death of initiation. Archetypal death and resurrection are important aspects of all great initiations— symbolically dying to the old and being reborn as a new self.

Eros revives her from her sleep and presents her as his desired bride to Zeus, his grandfather and the father of the gods. Psyche's symbolic death and rebirth mark the successful conclusion of her initiation. She attains her illumination and wins her place among the gods as a goddess and the wife of Eros.

The Primitive Brain

When you fail to complete one of your initiations, one of the seven deadly emotions begins to stir in primitive regions of your brain. For example, lust arises, and your mind then wraps a melodramatic story around this emotion, breathing substance into it and causing it to take on a life of its own. To understand the role of emotions, it's useful to distinguish them from feelings. When someone cuts in front of you on the highway, you get upset at that driver. Your spontaneous reaction of anger is a *feeling* that passes because your nervous system resets itself. Neurobiologists at Duke University Medical Center have discovered molecular "reset switches" that allow neurons in the brain to adapt to and recover from changes in the environment.[2]

Feelings are authentic. By contrast, emotions are like viruses infecting our primitive neurocomputer. If you're still angry days or years after an upsetting incident, what you're experiencing isn't a feeling but an *emotion* stored in a neural network. You rationalize this emotion, and you come to believe, for example, that your spiteful behavior toward your boss is justified and feel you have a right to be angry and wrathful.

Destructive and debilitating as they can be, our emotions once served an important survival purpose. In prehistoric times, survival often required behaviors such as taking from a neighbor, betraying a friend, and hoarding food. The Sawi tribe in Indonesia valued treachery and betrayal as one of the most admired deeds you could accomplish, and even had a notion of "fattening with friendship" persons whom they would prepare to eat in a cannibalistic feast. When Christian missionaries arrived in the 1950s and brought with them the story of the passion of Christ, they found that the villagers were completely bored by the narrative until the part of Judas, at which point they all paid rapt attention.[3]

Today, our archaic emotions are no longer helpful, and every religion teaches that we must resist them. Christianity instructs us to practice temperance, or self-control; when someone strikes us, we should "turn the other cheek" (not seek revenge), and we must love not only our neighbors but our enemies, too. Islam teaches control of anger, aggression, and quarreling. Buddhism calls for compassion and loving-kindness. Hinduism extols nonviolence and peace. Yet history has shown that these wise teachings have done little to restrain humanity's brutish instincts. They did not prevent the brutal Crusades waged against non-Christians, the Nazis' atrocious efforts to exterminate the Jews, the violence between Muslims and Hindus or Israelis and Arabs, or the torture of enemy combatants by soldiers from the armies of the so-called civilized world.

Shamans believe you cannot experience peace outwardly unless you recognize how violence can arise within yourself. Mother Teresa is said to have gone to serve the poor in Calcutta not because of a great spiritual calling, but because she discovered the Hitler within her. The shaman knows that you won't be able to turn the other cheek simply because you've heard about Jesus' commandment, or practice compassion because you've read a book by the Dalai Lama. Only through initiation, through facing your demons and defanging them, can you learn the lessons these primitive emotions have to teach you and transform their negative power into fuel that can be used by the higher brain.

During his initiation, Jesus went into the desert to confront his demons. In the course of your initiation, you meet your darkness and then shake off these shadowy emotions as an antelope shakes off its fear after narrowly escaping the lion. Then you can harvest the seven virtues of the higher brain.

Immersion

Once, when I was doing research in the South American rainforest, the shaman I was with suggested that I spend a night alone at the sandy shore of a tributary of the Amazon River. His one instruction was not to build a fire, because it would keep the animals away and prevent me from being fully immersed in the experience of the rainforest in the darkness.

That night, I experienced the jungle as a terrifying music box. Sound carried for miles. After sunset, the melody of the evening songbirds was replaced by the grunts of the howler monkeys. Soon, it became pitch black. The canopy of the forest blocked out the stars, and there was no moon. I could not even see my hand in front of my face.

I began to hear branches snapping nearby. I was convinced a jaguar was closing in on me and would make me its evening meal. I could feel my heart pounding, my palms sweating, and my body tensing itself to run blindly into the night. I tried to turn on my flashlight, but the batteries were gone. The old Indian had taken them! A frozen eternity went by as I listened to the rustling of branches drawing nearer. Then I reached into my pocket for the pack of matches I always carried with me. My hands shook so badly that I could not strike the light. I thought I could smell the creature that was stalking me, until I realized it was the smell of my own fear. Finally, as the head of the matchstick burst into flame, I saw a startled and terrified tree monkey staring at me from a few feet away.

I spent the entire night imagining every horrible way to die in the jungle, and whenever I dozed off, I was awakened by dreams of giant snakes. The following morning, when my mentor came for me, I was angry and exhausted, and accused him of irresponsibly putting me in harm's way. He looked at me with a smile and said, "The most annoying creatures here are the bugs."

The next time I went out alone into the rainforest at night, I allowed myself to experience anxiety in every cell of my body, to completely immerse myself in it. I noticed as my palms began to sweat and my heart to pound. I kept the attention on my body instead of imagining what might be out there. I was surprised that after a while, instead of being consumed by my despair, a part of my awareness was able to separate from it and witness my experience. I felt myself becoming calm. Images from my childhood appeared in my mind, reminding me of the past times I had experienced fear, and I bathed these images with the feeling of safety that I felt. At last a deep peace settled within me, and I could enjoy the symphony of the rainforest.

The Initiation

All emotions are viral programs running in the subconscious recesses of our brain. And every emotion creates suffering for ourselves and pain for others. *Feelings* are new, fresh, and of the moment. *Emotions* are old, tired, and programmed into neural networks in the archaic brain. We believe that we cry because we're sad or lash out because we're angry, but in reality these emotions arise from the depths and grab hold of us: we're sad because we cry, we're afraid because we flee, and we're angry because we strike. The belief that we cry because we're sad arises because we've wrapped a sentimental and false story around that emotion. Once we recognize emotions as viruses in our primitive neurocomputer, we can choose not to use them as our primary response to disconcerting situations. Then we'll cry when we are happy, when we are sad, or for no reason whatsoever.

Unfortunately, we learn to cling tightly to our dark emotions and the behaviors they generate, finding ways to justify and even ennoble them. In the West, greed is good, lust is essential for advertising, and fear sells life insurance and puts politicians in power. Despite all our self-help books, we haven't discovered how to liberate ourselves from our disempowering emotions and access the seven angelic qualities of our higher brain.

EXERCISE: Dissolving Emotions

Acknowledging that his true demons are within, the shaman knows what to do when his emotions take hold of him. He enters a state of awareness in which he experiences raw, pure emotion, then allows it to detach from his story. Once the emotion has dissipated, there is no longer "sad," there is only crying. There is no longer "scared," there is only running. By separating the emotion from the story, he transforms the destructive forces that, unchecked, would eat away at him. Try this practice the next time you feel anger at someone or something or lust after something you would like to have. Experience pure anger without the story of why you are furious, or who you are angry at. Experience pure lust without directing it at someone or something. When you experience pure anger or lust, it soon dissipates. Experience pure envy and desire, without the tale of why this person or that dress or this house would make you happy. When you experience pure envy, devoid of the story attached to it, it soon dissipates. As soon as the emotion dissolves, call in the angel of peace, of courage, or compassion, and allow this feeling to wash over you.

The initiation process breaks up the old emotions, along with their habits and behaviors, washing away the long-established neural pathways in your primitive brain like a flood sweeping away the roads. You become free of the debilitating grip of emotions and are able to experience pure *feeling* once again. You create new pathways in your brain—this time, for compassion, peace, and generosity. Shamans refer to this practice metaphorically as acquiring your eagle wings. You are able to soar above situations without becoming entangled in them. After you install one of the seven higher qualities, you look back at a memory of a painful experience through new eyes and discover the lessons it taught you. Each time you consciously decide to replace your anger with compassion toward self and others, every time you replace your hurt and pride with the powerful force of humility, you lay down new pathways in your brain. You bring in the angels of the higher self.

After the rewiring of your primitive emotional brain has begun, you stop denying your dark emotions or being consumed by them, and simply allow yourself to feel their mighty force, devoid of any story about why you are entitled to feel that way. You observe the shift within you as this energy transforms and leads you to the shores of your destination.

For initiation to be authentic, you can't rationalize your emotions away. Talking yourself out of your rage in the moment is expedient, but it isn't healing. You must experience how this demon of anger can possess every cell in your body. Feel its power. As you discern the pure anger inside of you, you'll notice that it begins to dissipate. Then, whenever you catch sight of the old pathway through the woods that you used to walk, you'll recall what happened on that road, but you won't relive the past. Memories will surface briefly, then your emotions will be carried away on the wind. You will walk a new path, one of grace and discovery. You will walk the path of the creators.

EXERCISE: Unearthing Your Stories

If you find that a powerful, dark emotion doesn't dissolve as you hold it in your awareness, it's because there's a deeper story attached to it that you must unearth. Sit with your lust or rage, and you will observe how its energy dissipates when you don't hold on to the story you attached to it. It becomes a pure sensation instead. If this does not happen after a minute or two, you must look deeper for the story or idea that lurks underneath the emotion. Then, like Mother Teresa, you'll find that it will lead you to your Calcutta, to your calling and creative expression. You will take what has been living in the shadows and bring it into the light, where it can be enlisted as an ally. Peace, generosity, and the higher qualities of the brain will arise naturally within you, lightening your load and uplifting you. You'll feel happy for no reason whatsoever.

To firmly install any of the seven new qualities into your life, you need to practice them. Thus, an essential part of initiation is to practice that quality starting immediately, reinforcing your new neural networks. You don't make plans to change. You change.

In one of the tales of the legendary King Arthur, the knights are sitting at their famous Round Table when the Holy Grail appears to them in a vision, covered in a shroud. As spiritual warriors, the knights recognize that this vision is a call from Spirit. They vow to find the Grail unveiled and agree to go in quest of it. They enter the forest, each knight at a place of his choosing, where it is darkest and there is no path. This tale is about the gifts we receive after we have defeated our negative emotions. The Grail appears to us, calling us on a quest. And we are no longer afraid to enter the dark forest, though we must do so at a place where there is no path—for had there been a path, the knights would have been following someone else's footsteps, and sure never to find the Holy Grail.

Masters Empowered by Initiation

Even during the darkest, most grim periods of human history, there were men and women who bravely managed to live illumined lives. They dwelled peacefully in lands often ruled by warlords who wielded the blade mercilessly. But instead of engaging in war, these individuals waged peace. When their towns were ravaged, they remained invisible to those who lived by the sword, and crafted a world of beauty and serenity even in the midst of conflict. In Asia, they were the monks who practiced the inner disciplines— the Chi Kung and Shaolin masters who moved through life with power and grace. In the Americas, they were the Laika, medicine men and women who eluded the Conquistadors who ravaged their land.

Laikas lived free from a European belief system about predators and prey, the loss of paradise, and the fall from grace. After the Conquest, many indigenous peoples of the Americas began to see themselves as stuck in a web of inevitable suffering. Yet after their initiation, they no longer felt the need to bemoan their fate or point a finger of blame upward at the gods or around them at their oppressors. They recognized that we inevitably experience tribulations, including such major ones as enslavement and the loss of culture. However, they also knew that we can orchestrate a different reality the moment we understand that divine order is conducting the symphony of creation, and we are playing an indispensable instrument as we make music with the heavens. Initiation allowed them to align themselves with that order to manifest harmony in their lives, in spite of oppressive outer circumstances. They became illumined, like Siddhartha, and joined the heavenly realm, like Psyche.

A shaman learned that responding to pain by looking around for the responsible party in order to exact revenge or demand justice simply caused more agony for everyone. He didn't waste precious energy perpetually contemplating the nature of his wounds or brandishing a sword at the shadows surrounding him. Instead, he spotted the wound, recognized its source, attended to healing

20

himself, and stayed alert to the danger of slipping back into the realm of predator and prey. He did this by shedding the story of the Conquest that once defined him and all his "problems," and by discovering the fresh new skin that lay underneath the old. Each morning, he renewed himself when he looked at his reflection in the lake.

Many of us are realizing that for all the counseling, workshops, and personal work we have done, we still feel drained by the endless battle against forces that appear to be external. We're seeing that we can't battle anger or greed or gluttony unless we devote every drop of our lifeblood to stamping it out. The "war" on drugs, cancer, or Wall Street greed is doomed to fail if, like the British who did not adjust to the new type of warfare in the American Revolution, we adhere to an obsolete mode of battle. We have discovered that the way to win the war is not through resistance but through acceptance and higher-order consciousness.

The shaman disassembles his hot buttons instead of trying to make the world stop pushing them. His courage and strength grow, tempering him like steel until one day he's able to say, "If I could live through that, I can live through anything." He has overcome his fear of death, the great final crossing. He has been initiated.

Points of Initiation

Instead of uprooting our anger, envy, gluttony, or sloth, most of us live in denial or ennoble these emotional demons until they grow so powerful that they manifest as physical illness, depression, the loss of a relationship, or some other disaster. In reality, these crises are a wake-up call to be initiated at last: to raise our level of consciousness and face our darkness—and our greatness—with eyes wide open.

You're most likely to immerse yourself in the process of initiation when you're feeling pushed to the edge. But why wait for disaster to strike before you accept this sacred transformation? Instead, you can confront your demons and call forth the angels of your higher self whenever you recognize that you're stuck in an emotional reaction that isn't working for you. When you ask yourself, "Why am I still so damned angry? I thought I worked through all this rage long ago," or "Why can't I be happy for him instead of constantly envying him because he has it so easy?" it's a sign you're called to initiation. The choice is yours. Avoid the temptation to brush away your realization that it's time for change.

Rites of Passage

Biological passages such as puberty and parenting were always enshrouded in ceremony and rituals in every culture. These rites provided a container for the feelings that run wild when we're letting go of childhood and taking up the mantle of adulthood, or bidding goodbye to our most vital and productive years and entering a quieter stage as an elder. Yet today we no longer practice rites of passage as the sacred transformations they were meant to be. We leave childhood kicking and screaming, and retire from our jobs when we're displaced by younger and more vital colleagues.

The desire to avoid the discomfort of change can cause us to hurry past these initiation points, skimming the surface of their meaning, reducing them to an excuse for a party. Consequently, the soul, in its longing to grow, will push us toward crisis points, bringing about a situation that will force us to leave behind the old toys and the worn-out ways of operating. Our soul brings us these crises to remind us that we don't have to remain stuck in the land of the hunters and the hunted. We are called to draw ourselves up to our full height and confidence, even when terrified at the prospect of the unknown.

In later chapters, you'll learn the shamans' tools for identifying and healing the emotions that are draining you, so that even the most challenging times don't plunge you into despair. You'll learn how to find the opportunities hidden in crisis, discover the flow of pure water from the source upstream, and explore with the wonder and curiosity of a creator. You'll recognize that however overwhelming your life may seem at any given moment, you'll make it through the dark woods and find your Holy Grail, that place of grace, wisdom, and power you've sought. But, like Siddhartha and Psyche, you will have to make the great departure from the familiar and plunge into the unknown. You will be challenged, and others will attempt to seduce you into returning to the old ways, to the comfort of the palace or the familiar role of the jilted lover. Your resolve will be tested, and you may lose everything you think you love, even your old life. But if you emerge successful, you will reap the bounty of the great awakening and enter into the rarefied heavenly realms, as Psyche did.

To change your emotional patterns, you must start by recognizing that you are living in a world of your own creation. You are the author of the dream or nightmare you are living. Only by recognizing this false reality, invented and perpetuated by your primitive brain, can you begin to break free of the spider's web and awaken the higher qualities of purity, love, compassion, and charity. Otherwise, these deadly demons will settle in your cells and tissue, creating physical and psychic disease, and blinding you to your path.

CHAPTER 2

The Hunter
and the Hunted

I have a job at a prestigious university. I direct my own research laboratory, where I study how the mind creates psychosomatic health or disease. I'm fascinated by the work, so it should be the ideal life—but it is miserable. Today, the dean of the biology department wants to see all the graded papers from one of my classes. Seems I gave out too many A's and B's and not enough D's. I am supposed to follow the bell curve.

The dean doesn't like the research I do, and he creates every possible obstacle for me. "Mind-body research belongs in the psychology department, not in biology," he says. "And your work smacks of spirituality." His disdain is palpable. But he needs the research money I bring in because it lets him justify his department's expenses to his superiors.

I am going to turn this meeting around. Put him on the defensive. I will threaten to take my lab to the psych department! Threats are the only language his primitive brain understands.

Journal
San Francisco

The seven deadly sins that have plagued humanity are part of our ancient survival hardware that reads the world as a hostile, predatory place where we have only two opposing choices: to eat or to be eaten.

Each time we open the newspaper or turn on the television, we can see clearly that we live in a world in which big fish swallow little fish, corporations and power structures gobble up the little guy, and pain overwhelms the intention to be kind. It's a world of "us" versus "them," where everyone is hunting or being hunted. This is the popularized version of evolutionary theory, introduced by Charles Darwin in his landmark book, *On the Origin of Species*.

Darwin proposed that since more individuals are born than can be supported by an ecosystem, the weakest will be eliminated in the struggle for existence. The fit will survive, and the survivors will pass on their traits to their offspring. The idea of the struggle for existence has been traced as far back as the 8th-century Afro-Arab scholar Al-Jahiz, whose carefully recorded observations of nature and human behavior seemed to anticipate the concept of natural selection. Yet new research in evolutionary biology suggests that there's another successful strategy for survival, one based on wisdom and cooperation. Simon Conway Morris, a paleontologist at Cambridge University, has observed how entirely different species evolved similar means for solving similar problems, and concluded that evolution has two trends: the quest for complexity and the search for intelligence. To ensure that the human race would have the greatest intelligence, the wisest and most cooperative would have to survive. Brute force and fierce competition are no longer the sole keys to survival.

Contrary to Darwinian concepts of evolution, in higher organisms evolution favors the most cooperative. Take honey bee colonies, for example, where workers collaborate for the common good. The human body works in much the same way. There are over 100 trillion cells in the body that survive not by competing with each other for available food in the bloodstream, but by working cooperatively as a colony. Yet humans as a species have yet to discover what bees know: the survival of the individual depends on the well-being of the hive.

When we perceive the world as only a competitive, hostile place, we can't help feeling nervous. If we were taught a literal reading of the Bible, we learn about an Old Testament God who has to be appeased with sacrifice, and who repeatedly destroys his own creatures, as He did with the sinners of Sodom and Gomorrah. Researcher Phil Zuckerman found that in countries where food is plentiful and health care widely available, fewer people believe in this type of demanding deity than in countries where people feel more insecure and existence is more precarious.[4] This research suggests that religious belief in a Supreme Being and rejection of evolutionary theory are found more often in those societies that are most subject to Darwinian forces of survival through competition. Many people still believe in the medieval notion that if we displease this all-powerful God, he will cast us down to the fires of the underworld, or bring plagues, bad luck, and illness upon us. This perception of God as a wrathful deity is the product of the primitive limbic brain. When we believe that such a deity is our Lord, we focus on gaining power in the material world, becoming little gods of our own making. We figure that if we amass enough wealth and reputation, we can stave off damnation and find some security.

However, once we understand how we are bound to a life of strife by the neural networks in the brain, we're no longer subject to the whims of a fickle celestial master and his demons or his fates, and we can instead discover spirituality for ourselves. We can find our power in the same way that Psyche and Siddhartha did, as co-creators in the realm of Creation, the alternative to the predatory world most people live in. And just as America was the first modern land where people could practice freedom of religion, perhaps someday America will be a place where we enjoy freedom *from* religion, and discover true spirituality through the awakening of our higher brain functions.

Two Realms or Realities

The belief in two very different realms—the realm of Spirit and the realm of the flesh—has been present throughout history. Philosophers, theologians, spiritual leaders, and scientists have suggested that there are perhaps even several simultaneous adjoining realities that we're capable of experiencing. Even Einstein, in his revolutionary equation $E = mc^2$, divided the physical universe into two parts, the side of energy and the side of matter. Physicists have discovered that universes parallel to ours may somehow influence and inform our own, even though the passageway to them may be through black holes from which nothing, not even light, can escape. The shaman recognizes that what most people call reality, the Darwinian world of hunter and hunted, of masters and slaves, and the Keynesian economics of scarcity, is not the only realm of existence. Alongside this world is the dwelling place of the creators—men and women who live in abundance and peace, an abode that we've named paradise or heaven. These two parallel worlds are separated by only the thinnest of veils. In neuroscience this veil is known as the corpus callosum, a structure in the brain that facilitates communication between our more primitive limbic brain and our neocortex, as well as between our left and right brain hemispheres.

"Paradise" need not be an idyllic state that we can only attain after death or favors from the gods. Nirvana, the Elysian Fields, and Valhalla of Norse legend are just around the corner. When Christ said that the "kingdom of God is within you" he suggested that it is within our reach right now. We can achieve paradise once we make a simple but crucial shift that awakens the faculties of our higher brain and the realization that we're a spark of the divine, always in concert with Spirit. There is nothing else that we can be. This realization is achieved only through illumination, not through study, penance, or prayer. It must be a spiritual experience, not simply an intellectual understanding of how the brain works or how peace is possible.

Paradise is where we see beauty while others see only ugliness, where we bring truth to places in which others only experience deceit, where we behave with integrity where others feel compelled to compromise, and where we take our place as co-creators amid the exquisite workings of the universe. This doesn't mean that disease, death, or war cease to exist, but that anger, fear, and illness are no longer perceived as the constants in our lives. The suspicion, competition, and violence we witness daily is the result of our being tethered to a world where kindness and goodness are trampled upon by greed and wrath, and we fight with each other to get a seat on the bus. However, paradise isn't separated from the "real world" by an impenetrable wall, but by a wispy and fluid membrane—a large, flat bundle of axons beneath the neocortex. We can allow paradise to seep through and offer us a new way of perceiving, characterized by courage, insight, joy, and creativity. After all, paradise is a brain state, not a place. When our base emotions are transformed into the higher neocortical qualities, a sense of expansiveness and possibility is created. We start to recognize that we can change the world with every thought we have and every word we speak. Feedback from the universe arrives instantaneously.

If we observe the natural world, the law of tooth and claw seems to be dominant, and we become convinced that there's only one reality—the predatory one. Richard Dawkins, a well-known evolutionary biologist, states, "The total amount of suffering per year in the natural world is beyond all decent contemplation. During the minute it takes me to compose this sentence, thousands of animals are being eaten alive; others are running for their lives, whimpering with fear; others are being slowly devoured from within by parasites; thousands of all kinds are dying of starvation, thirst and disease. It must be so. If there is ever a time of plenty, this very fact will automatically lead to an increase in population until the natural state of starvation and misery is restored."[5] Indeed, in the wild, the relationship between predator and prey strikes a delicate balance. Even the animals at the top of the food chain become nourishment for the lowliest bacteria. Nothing remains the same: creatures are born, age, and die, and flowers bloom and fade until they finally decay, while their pollen germinates other flowers or becomes the honey that sustains the beehive.

This is true. The world of creators is not a Camelot-like fantasyland where lions are vegetarians and humans are always kind. Life continues to feed on itself, but your life is not a conjugation of the verb "to eat" but a conjugation of the verb "to create."

Rejects from Paradise

When did we begin to perceive the predatory world and all its limitations as the only reality and the world of creative possibilities as the fantasy? According to the Bible, the first humans lived in paradise. With no regrets about the past or fears about tomorrow, they strolled through Eden, exploring its riches, eating its fruits, and living in harmony with all creatures, from the tiniest microbe to the most fearsome carnivore. Then they got themselves cast out of the land of abundance and into a world of scarcity where hunter and prey struggled endlessly for domination and survival. After the Fall, man had to live by the sweat of his brow, harvesting the thorns and thistles that the earth produces, while woman was condemned to give birth in pain. After spending many years in the Amazon Rainforest, I still marvel at how abundant the fruit of our earthly garden really is. I have seldom ever encountered thorns and thistles, and when I did, they were more than offset by the mangos and papayas.

The Book of Genesis describes the first great initiation humans faced and how, alas, we failed to meet the challenge presented to us by God. Adam and Eve ate the forbidden fruit on the advice of the serpent, who assured them it would impart knowledge, not death as God had warned. Although Christian theology equates the serpent with Satan, ancient traditions saw the snake as a symbol of fertility and renewal, or as a wise trickster; so the serpent's advice seems to contain some positive potential. Indeed, once they took that bite, Adam and Eve broke out of their identity as naive children and began their journey of initiation into manhood and womanhood. They had the opportunity to become powerful adults, joining the Creator in fashioning a dynamic world of beauty and grace. In fact, in the next verse the Lord admits, "The man has now become like one of us, knowing good and evil."

Instead of stepping confidently into their new identities, Adam and Eve hesitated, fearful of God's wrath and the change they had wrought. Just as they were waking up to the neocortical awareness of good and evil, their primitive brain made them ashamed of their nakedness, their vulnerability, and their sexual desire. They hid from the Lord, who would surely punish them, they believed. Instead of reaching out to "take also from the tree of life, and eat, and live forever," they collapsed into the lower-brain emotions of wrath, envy, and pride. Unlike Psyche and Siddhartha, who attained their immortality, our mythical ancestors failed to attain illumination. They were banished from the Garden and felt deeply ashamed, and accepted that suffering and death would be their lot, and their children's lot until the end of time.

In certain Native American myths, the story of creation reads differently. Indigenous people are not banished from Eden; they are given the Garden in order to be its stewards and caretakers. Spirit invites humans to embrace their creator attributes, and says: "For I made the butterflies and the salmon and the deer . . . Aren't they beautiful? Now you finish the job of creation." The shaman is honored to be granted the privilege of completing the job by taking up the role of co-creator.

A Story of Incomplete Initiation

The story of Adam and Eve is a myth of initiation gone awry, and it's partly responsible for our fixation with psychological "father issues." In the story, our primordial parents are parted from their "father" when he banishes them from paradise. Although psychologists would say that every child must go through such separation and loss of innocence to become an independent individual, it is a myth that has kept us disempowered and in bondage. Unlike the hero who willingly embarks on a great and difficult journey, Adam and Eve were cast out in shame.

Western mythology is founded on a story of failed initiation and has left us bereft of a model of how we can attain our illumination, like the Buddha or like Psyche. The myth also illustrates the price we pay when we fail to complete an initiation. Adam and Eve didn't eat of the fruit of the second tree, of life everlasting, which would have given them freedom from death, like the gods. They missed their prize, and that aborted initiation continues to haunt us to this day. According to Christian theologians, every child is born with the mark of "original sin" inherited from Adam and Eve, which causes him or her to be vulnerable to the seven demons of anger, greed, lust, sloth, envy, gluttony, and pride.

With such a mythic story of the hardships of initiation defining the Western human adventure, it's no wonder we feel pessimistic about life and conclude that we live in a dog-eat-dog world. But the biblical story of Genesis leaves us with a message of hope for salvation and an eventual return to paradise. Yet many of us resign ourselves to the cynical view that happiness and peace on earth are elusive and that the universe is conspiring against us. We despair of ever finding solutions to a never-ending string of troubles.

Some look to a supernatural being for rescue, while others grasp at whatever security can be acquired in the material world, from money to reputation to power. Others resort to denial, willpower, workaholism, and a multitude of distractions to ease their suffering. They overlook the possibility that we might have the power to discover paradise through the process of illumination available to all who undergo their initiations in a mythic and sacred manner.

Finding Our Genuine Power

The seven emotions of the primitive brain may appear to give us power within a predatory world. Accumulating things gives us a sense of stability. Overeating gives us a sense of satiation. Looking fierce gets us what we want. Lusting after a better partner or job gives us a sense of purpose. Soon, however, we feel sucked dry by our adversarial relationship with life. These emotions leach our vitality, and we become worn out by the battle to attain psychological, financial, and physical security. We try to de-stress or meditate but have too many things on our mind. We're left longing for peace for ourselves and understanding from others.

The shaman knows that there's a way to conquer these demons. Her weapon is a sword of light, which represents the power of higher reason and deep insight, and exposes these demons as archaic parts of ourselves that we disown and project onto others. What we slash away at externally—by fighting with our spouse, or blaming and criticizing people we abhor—is merely a reflection of the demons within, the "shadow side" buried deep in our unconscious. Carl Jung, the originator of archetypal psychology, believed that confronting our personal shadow is a moral challenge comparable to facing the very problem of human evil itself. The shaman is confident that by withdrawing our projections, consciously owning our shadow, and experiencing the toxic emotions without acting on them, we transform their energy into fuel to change ourselves for the better. Thus, in a phrase attributed to Gandhi, we *become* the change we want to see in the world.

Cleansing the Emotions

During initiation, you confront deadly emotions as they rear their ugly heads. You allow them to wash through every cell in your body in their purest form, without projecting that story onto others. You experience pure wrath, not rage directed at someone who you believe has wronged you. You experience pure lust, not lust directed at a person or thing you crave. As you cease denying these emotions, you can begin to understand the wisdom they have to offer you, because when they are not attached to people and objects, they quickly wash through you. When we release attachment to the object of anger or desire, there is no more suffering. This experience will rewire your neural networks and allow you to experience the higher qualities that are the counterparts of the deadly emotions. Unless you own and befriend the extraordinary power of your emotions, and the stories we create and project onto others, you can't change the wiring in your brain. You read spiritual books and believe that you're incapable of hurting a fly, when in reality you are sitting with a sword drawn on your lap, ready to chop off heads. But when you learn to master this power, you emerge from the predatory world of unconscious emotions and projections and return to paradise.

One Reality, Two Brains

The two worlds—that of hunter and hunted, and the world of paradise—are versions of the same reality perceived by two very different structures of the brain. The primitive brain, which we share with all mammals, with the Great Apes (chimps, orangutans, gorillas), and with our extinct relatives the Neanderthals, is concerned exclusively with physical and emotional survival and perceives the world as predatory. This brain perceives danger and threat everywhere, believes that good fences make good neighbors, and stockpiles rocks, just in case our neighbor ever breaks down our fence. This brain crafted our recently discarded nuclear deterrence policy nicknamed MAD, or mutual assured destruction.

The more recently evolved neocortex ("new brain") is able to perceive a world where we tear down fences and reduce nuclear stockpiles, and where people collaborate toward peace and sustainable lifestyles. Our new brain can even experience realms that transcend the ordinary senses, through ideas such as democracy, science, art, and spirituality, and the understanding that your consciousness can never be extinguished.

The more we learn about how the brain perceives the world, the more we understand the notion of heaven being at hand, and the easier it is for us to envision the end of suffering that the Buddha described. Removing the overlay of religion from these wisdom teachings, we can look at them from the perspective of neuroscience and begin to understand why it's so difficult for us to surrender to our divine, higher nature. While our neocortex invites us to reason, make love, and write music and poetry, we are still dominated by our more instinctive brain. When little Suzy is called on by her teacher to read out loud in front of the class, her limbic brain may not be able to distinguish between this scary prospect and being bullied by other children on the school steps. When the prehistoric brain is in charge of consciousness, we scramble like furry creatures competing according to the laws of the jungle.

While working as a psychologist during graduate school, I treated an eight-year-old named Tristan, who was quick to anger and used his fists instead of words. I explained to him about the "feeling brain" and the "thinking brain," and he immediately understood. One day, he said to me, "My feeling brain is like my dad, who gets out of bed quickly in the morning. But my thinking brain is like my mom, who likes to sleep in, and it's hard to wake her up sometimes."

The primitive brain is focused on the four F's of survival— feeding, fornicating, fighting, and fleeing. Within this brain lies the amygdala, an almond-shaped structure responsible for the instantaneous response to a perceived threat. The amygdala switches on the sympathetic nervous system, which gives us the energy to face our adversaries or outrun them, and shuts down higher cortical function. When Tristan's teacher called on him, he froze and wanted to run out of the room. His higher brain functions were shut down momentarily, and all he could think about was fight or flight. Next to the amygdala is the hippocampus, which is involved in storing and accessing emotionally rich memories. Our brain then attributes meaning to these emotions, where we turn "I feel lonely" into "Why did my father abandon me?" The hippocampus is like a stadium full of cheerleaders who get excited at every play of the amygdala. Yet there are no real spectators in the stadium, no one with an unbiased sense of reality, only the cheerleaders who are eagerly looking for something to trumpet.

How Our Neural Networks Determine Our Experience of Reality

For small children, each new experience is truly novel, setting the coordinates that map out their reality. Our minds are so malleable at this stage in human development that the Jesuits used to say, "Give me the child until he is seven, and I will give you the man." By age seven, our neural pathways begin to associate each new experience with something that happened in the past. That pathway for "abandonment," "disrespect," or "betrayal" lights up the moment something happens that seems to match up with our previous experience. What we see is what we expect to see: evidence that the emotions generated by our neural networks are justified. It's like the story of the two travelers who meet on the road, and the first traveler asks what kind of people he can expect to meet in the next town. The second traveler asks him what the people were like in the town he just left. "The place was full of thieves, and there was not a single honest man in town." The second traveler looks at him and says: "Well, those are exactly the kind of people you will meet in the next town."

Of course, not all our early experiences are emotionally charged. In fact, all events are neutral—we're the ones who assign them a quality. When we see people suffering, we can choose to get in touch with our humanity and feel a strong desire to make a difference in the world, or we can look at the same scene and say, "Isn't that always how it is? Life sucks." In theory, while the circuitry for pleasure and pain are available since birth, the operating system for joy will not be available until the neocortex is fully online. With this awareness, we could live truly original lives and perceive that the world is fine just as it is in any moment. Unfortunately, we have to earn this privilege.

As parents, we inevitably guide our children into conforming to the social values of our group. We instinctively know that they need support from others in order to survive, and that they're more likely to receive it if they're seen as nonthreatening "team players." As children are taught to tailor their behavior to the expectations of those around them, the brain begins to prune the neural pathways that aren't necessary for thriving in their culture. A Chinese baby does not need the synapses that allow it to distinguish between the spoken sounds of the English letters L and R, while an American baby does not need the ones that help it distinguish between an explosive P and a nonexplosive one (a sound that doesn't appear in spoken English). And a five-year-old who learns from her mother that she can't trust her dad to be around will eventually develop neural networks that support the belief that she cannot trust men.

Because of this process, known as synaptic pruning, the child's ability to have pure, original experiences begins to diminish. Between the ages of 7 and 15, we lose 80 percent of our synaptic connections—along with the many alternative ways of perceiving the world and the creativity this inspires. The more conditional a child's parents' love is, the more limited his creative response to the world will become. When my children were young and I took them to the park, I remember overhearing many well-meaning parents call out to their children and reward them with a big smile and a comment of "that's a good boy." The message the child receives is that his parents' affections are hinged upon good behavior. As they grew older, my children learned that getting good grades and behaving meant that they were doing their best—not for my approval but for their own sense of pride.

The neocortex can consciously understand events and change our feelings about them. We are able to have an experience and choose not to associate it with the vague emotion that suddenly arises. We can say, "Ah, there I go again, getting irritated when someone ignores my needs." However, the instant emotional eruptions will hijack our higher-level reasoning every time a similar circumstance presents itself.

One way to get neurons firing together into new networks is through meditation, a calm state from which we can observe or witness the emotional mind as it chatters away. Another is to practice the seven virtues of the neocortex. But changing our emotional habits isn't nearly as easy as we'd like it to be. An event that someone else might experience as benign instead becomes connected to a memory of having been hurt, falsely accused, or betrayed. The amygdala makes lightning-quick associations, categorizing a new event as a dangerous repetition of an old trauma. Each time we experience something that resembles a case of abandonment, betrayal, or manipulation, the amygdala shouts, "I know what that's about!" and automatically sets off the alarms and assigns current meaning to the memory before we have a chance to think our way through it. Conscious reflection is an afterthought, an attempt to understand a lightning-fast response from primitive regions of our brain.

Whenever we experience anger, pain, fear, envy, and sadness, the old neural networks become reinforced like a well-worn path through a field. We become blind to all other possibilities and get stuck on the same old road to heartache. Unable to take charge of how we interpret our experiences, the new brain relinquishes control, only coming back online later to try to make sense of what just happened. I remember once getting so angry with my son that I thought I could understand why sometimes lions eat their young! And then a few minutes later I was puzzled and confused as to how I could have felt such rage at the person whom I loved the most in this life.

When we're driven by our deadly emotions, we see only through the lens of suspicion and distrust. The faculties of the neocortex are then enlisted to dominate others in order to stay ahead, instead of being employed to make music or a scientific discovery. Although the neocortex understands the power of logic and reason, it's so busy sorting through the emotional data brought into awareness by the limbic brain that it devotes almost all of its energy to figuring out how to stop all the suffering. Our lives become about explaining our problems and strategizing to fix them, to avoid more pain.

Man the Hunter

The monkey's instincts direct him to scramble up a tree when the scent of a jaguar on the prowl reaches his nostrils. Fortunately, it's not in his nature to sit in the branches endlessly pondering why he must put so much effort into surviving in a world where safety can never be taken for granted. Unlike monkeys and apes, we have a highly developed "new" brain that can plan; predict; communicate ideas; and conceive of poetry, art, and music—and that has allowed us to rise to the top of the food chain. Yet that same complex brain also readily succumbs to the belief that life is an endless and depressing series of challenges to be overcome. The monkey who has outmaneuvered the jaguar rests and then turns to the next task at hand, whether it's grooming or eating. His fear is short-lived, a feeling that dissipates as the danger disappears. In contrast, we respond to our narrow escapes by depositing that feeling into the bank account of an old neural pathway. We agonize about how overwhelming all this chasing and escaping, feeding, and hunting can be. We breathe life into our fear and write poems about it. Misery becomes our muse.

As we analyze our difficulties, we start to feel kicked around by a universe that doesn't seem to care very much about us. The most recently evolved parts of our brain, the prefrontal cortex, usually remain dormant throughout this self-imposed misery. This is the region of the brain that can envision and manifest a different reality. If it does awaken by accident, an experience of psychosis can result, presenting us with the question of which world is real: am I having lunch with my beloved, or I am being eaten for lunch? This brain and its facility to dream our world differently is available to everyone, but for it to be a healthy one, we must have broken free of the power the seven deadly emotions have over us.

As we contemplate the existence of a Supreme Being, we imagine that he is overseeing this interplay of hunter and hunted, and must have some excellent tips for winning the dangerous game of survival. After all, he's truly at the top of the food chain. We plead and bargain with him to give us an edge over the competition, but he is silent. Frustrated, we set aside our integrity, and reason that this compromise is the price we have to pay in order to win. We aspire to emulate the angry sky god who throws thunderbolts and smites his enemies, and who insists that we do the same if we're to have any hope of gaining power over the world.

But at the end of the day, as darkness overtakes the sky, we gaze into the fire and wonder. The endless battle and the perpetual hunt for nourishment drains us of our joy, our passion, and our hope. The thought of preparing a new résumé, opening up another credit card bill, suffering through another painful interaction with the sibling we've been fighting with since childhood, or spending yet another uncomfortable evening with our spouse trying to hash out the problems in our relationship makes us feel like the hollow shell of an insect left hanging in the web after the spider has devoured its insides.

Discover Your Power

You have the power to release yourself from the primitive brain programming that makes you think it rains to make you wet, that the reason you're so angry is that someone took your parking spot, or that your childhood is the source of your problems. The only person who can serve as your programmer is you. But first you must change your notion of God as the ultimate rescuer who can be wooed, appeased, and coaxed into saving you from suffering. In fact, you must drop the notion of God altogether, because it is a uniquely human creation. Would humans be so privileged as to be the only creatures capable of perceiving God? We're as capable of comprehending Creation as a group of baboons are capable of understanding quantum theory. You are the only one who can lift yourself out of this bleak reality.

The shaman recognizes that, like everyone, she has a spark of the Divine but is not the fire itself. Still, she realizes that the vast beauty of the universe can be understood through direct experience, which both humbles her and makes her able to correct the harsh reality perceived by the limbic brain. She willingly participates in crafting a reality of trust rather than fear, of joy rather than anger and sorrow.

Most of us were raised to believe in a supernatural force and taught that faith without evidence was particularly noble. We learn that those who believe without seeing are blessed. Western religions teach that it's the role of priests and church authorities to interpret God's will and relay to us his intent. Certain that they understand divine revelation, they instruct us on how to remain in God's good graces and avoid the plagues and calamities that befall others. The commandments they teach can help us avoid the worst suffering caused by living in a predatory world, but they don't necessarily awaken us to an awareness of our role in Creation. Too often, religion reinforces the neocortex's submission to the primitive limbic brain and its emotionally driven behaviors. After all, most of the wars being fought around the planet today are religious in nature.

The first and most difficult task of the shaman is to break the spell of believing without seeing. She opens her eyes and sees that the palace is a prison, or the prison a palace. This is the stage of awakening. Then she must seek her own initiation. Jesus, after his initiation, said, "Even greater things than I have done, you shall do." The shaman does away with notions of a supernatural god and then takes up residence in the world of creators, while recognizing the presence of Spirit all about.

As a shaman, you have the potential to bring about your own everyday miracles and draw on your reservoir of personal power, which will sustain you through unexpected challenges in life. A job loss, bankruptcy, or any other crisis is an opportunity for you to reconnect with your passion and purpose, to be surprised and even delighted by what you find. Surrendering to the possibilities lying on the other side of the passage, you may even use the opportunity to realize that this hardscrabble life is only one reality—and a pretty sorry one at that.

One of my clients, after being diagnosed with breast cancer, found the courage to undergo her initiation at several levels. When chemotherapy made her hair fall out, she went out and bought red, blond, and brunette wigs that were fun to wear. She realized that her intense stress reactions to a grueling job and the departure from home of her grown children may have contributed to her vulnerability to illness. All of this was challenging enough, but then she also had the courage to see the cancer as an opportunity to rise up from the living death she'd been enduring in a long-term relationship that had just ended badly. She was willing to heal not just physically but also in her very soul, and she went back to school as she began to fashion a new life for herself. Two years later, she was cancer-free and had a new degree in hand. When one of her friends asked her if she was afraid of having to start all over again in a new career at age 50, she smiled and said she was as happy as a young college grad. But like Psyche, she had to make her own journey through the underworld, meeting her many fears and demons, to retrieve the splendid potion that would help her feel the beauty in and around her.

Recognizing that we can dwell in the world of innovators, we live daringly. Illness is no longer an enemy but an opportunity. We can let go of the primitive instinct that causes us to imagine that every situation that startles or upsets us is a sign of danger. If we can do this, we'll find that we have taken the route of initiation and surrendered to the vast, dark abyss of the unknown. Our reservoir of power allows us to open ourselves to whatever will be, take a deep gulp from the canteen, and say to ourselves, "Well, I'm not sure where I'm going, but it should be an interesting trip."

The woods we walk through on our journey to initiation may appear to be dark and dangerous, and the tales of feral cats and poisonous snakes will ring in our ears. But when we recall that we're the one who spun those scary stories around the campfire, we can stop running in fear and remember that we are brave, powerful, and inventive.

CHAPTER 3

Taming the Prehistoric Brain

I've always been fascinated by the scientific fact that the limbic brain cannot tell the difference between a real and a perceived event. This is why, for example, visualizing that you are lying in the sunshine on a beautiful beach can bring as much relaxation as actually being there. This fact also explains why public rituals allow a community to bring to the surface and heal hidden feelings of hurt or aggression. For instance, the Roman Catholic Mass, with its symbolic transformation of anguish and torment into the joy of Christ's resurrection, can provide release from the personal internal suffering of the individuals who attend the sacrament. The Kabuki theater of Japan is another type of public ritual. I've read that Kabuki originated in the early 1600s as a form of comedy, but after the disgrace endured by the Japanese after their defeat in World War II, the style of Kabuki performers became rigid, constrained, and stiff, with truncated movements that expressed the nation's painful loss of dignity. Similarly, shamanic rituals allow the brain to acknowledge and work through painful emotions in an archetypal way.

Journal

The human brain is made up of four anatomically different subcomputers that developed over millions of years of evolution. The most ancient one is the *reptilian brain*, which we share with lizards and dinosaurs. This brain is programmed to breathe, eat, and breed. Enveloping and informing it is the *limbic brain*, which I have variously called the mammalian brain, and the lower or primitive brain. We share the limbic system with the Neanderthals, our now-extinct prehistoric relatives, as well as with other primates and all mammals. The limbic brain helps us to do an even more sophisticated job of survival, allowing us to store nuts or roots for the winter, recognize predators, and bond with others to form families and tribes. It's the limbic brain that causes us to want shelter and protect our loved ones, that helps us learn things by rote, and to sniff out food that has spoiled or "smell" danger.

The limbic brain is the brain of beliefs and emotions. There is nothing cuddly about a snake, which lacks a limbic brain, but a puppy, who is able to respond to feelings and emotions, is utterly lovable. This primitive brain gets pumped up for battle, lusts after your neighbor's spouse, shows no mercy to a weaker opponent, and sucks up to those you consider wealthier or more powerful than you. The limbic brain's programs so strongly influence our behavior that five out of the Ten Commandments are mandates to rein in our primitive instincts—killing, adultery, stealing, bearing false witness, and coveting. As the source of all beliefs about the nature of life, the limbic brain allowed us to invent religion. It also generates every limiting belief we hold about ourselves, including our low self-esteem, self-doubt, guilt about sexuality, and fear of scarcity.

The *neocortex* is our new brain—the most recent part of the brain to evolve. This is the brain of knowledge and science that scoffs at beliefs, insisting instead on hypotheses that can be tested out against reality. I like this old joke about the difference between science and religion: With science, you develop a hypothesis and test it out against the facts. If the facts prove it wrong, you throw away the hypothesis and come up with a better one. With religion, you take a hypothesis and test it out against the facts—and if the facts prove it wrong, you throw away the facts! This is why, when you're arguing with someone, no amount of facts that support your position will help you win. The primitive brain gives more weight to circumstantial evidence and what one believes to be true than to the truth itself.

We share the neocortex with other mammals, but in humans its many folds enable it to be larger and capable of more advanced cognitive skills. The human neocortex thus added language and speech to our survival repertoire. This brain comprehends time, the seasons, as well as past and future, giving us the capacity for foresight. It is also responsible for poetry and music, which, although of no great survival value in the African savannah, were the ingredients for a future wisdom society and for survival of the wisest—the merchants, craftspeople, pyramid architects, scientists, and scribes. With the development of the neocortex, it was not the ablest hunter who got the most fertile females, the most land, or the most shekels, but the smartest one.

Each of these three sub-brains—the reptilian brain, the limbic brain, and the neocortex—can be thought of as a holon (from the Greek word *holos,* meaning "whole"), a unit that is complete within itself and also a part of a larger organic structure. All of these brains perform their biologically programmed functions, yet they submit to the guidance of the highest brain, in the same way that our stomach has its job but does not set the agenda for our day. The term "hierarchy" isn't quite right for the interrelationship of parts of the brain, because it doesn't reflect the feedback that occurs in a living system; *holarchy* better expresses the fact that the lower brains often inform the higher brains rather than simply obeying them. Holons are autonomous, self-reliant units that handle local decision making without asking higher authorities for instructions. The reptilian brain has to continue regulating breathing and body temperature automatically, while the mammalian brain has to seek partnerships without making the search for relationships our only goal. Likewise, the neocortex offers us the ability to reason, to think logically, and to discover music and science, without making our lives revolve around technology or be limited by our intellect. All of these brains serve the higher agenda of the fourth brain, the *prefrontal area* of the neocortex, which is the system's integrator of our biological supercomputer.

When one of these sub-brains is traumatized by emotional or environmental factors, its programs will override the agendas of the higher brains. So, if you experienced hunger when you were young, forced to go to bed some nights with a growling, empty stomach, it's likely that your instinctive limbic brain will play a strong role in setting your agenda.

Suppose a child doesn't bond with his mother in the first year of life; the holarchy will be compromised, and its seven demons will be let loose from their lairs. The four F's will take over the neural apparatus: fear, feeding, fighting, and fornicating will run amok. In a study of tribal cultures around the world, James Prescott, Ph.D., from the Institute of Humanistic Science found that it's possible to predict with 80 percent accuracy the peaceful or homicidal tendencies of all societies based on a single factor: mother-child bonding.[6] Specifically, this bonding involves continuously carrying the baby close to its mother (or a surrogate) for the first year of life. Premodern societies understood this instinctively, and today in the highlands of Peru or the rice paddies of Thailand, you can still see women with their babies slung on their backs or strapped to their chests as they work in the fields. Our life in the modern world no longer permits this degree of intimate contact and bonding between mother and child. And thus our limbic brain no longer feels we are safe, wanted, or worthy.

When the prefrontal cortex is in charge of the holarchy, we're able to experience how we are interwoven with and inseparable from the rest of the universe. With this brain, we understand there's more to life than mere survival and existence, more than just consumption, hoarding, and technological toys. We can apprehend this only if this most recently evolved brain takes the driver's seat of the neural machinery. Shamans of the past understood this intuitively, without comprehending the way the brain works. They devised ways of attaining higher brain functions through the process of initiation.

Initiation helps us heed the prefrontal cortex's call for beauty and creativity, which is too easily drowned out by the everyday demands of the lower brains. When preoccupied with survival, the primitive brain will protect its agenda, unaware that its seven resident demons can turn on us and devour us. Greed becomes all-consuming, anger eats away at us, and pride becomes our downfall unless we can establish the proper holarchy of awareness, allowing the higher brain to guide our thoughts, feelings, and actions.

Psychologists in the early 1900s developed complex theories to explain the origins of depression, psychosis, and other mental illnesses. Yet the talking cures have proven to be of dubious value. Our early parental wounds brought us in touch with our inner child, a child we believed we could nurture, but who soon turned into a petty dictator. Higher-order thinking cannot prevail when all we perceive is scarcity and danger, and we think our purpose is to fix our problems and ease our suffering. We forget about exploring love and freedom, and opening ourselves to joy, wonder, and mystery, even as we continue to work on bettering our lives.

Reprogramming Neural Networks

If the stories of angels and demons battling it out for your soul don't resonate with you, you might think of their opposing forces in a less poetic way, using the language of brain science. Each of us has neural pathways in our brain—functionally and chemically connected neurons—that are created when neurons that fire together then wire together. These networks act as information superhighways that reinforce the beliefs that lead us to act angrily, greedily, and lustfully in order to guard against perceived threats to our survival. Remember that the limbic brain functions with beliefs about reality, while the new brain works with theories that it tests out against reality.

To reprogram these information superhighways, we have to eject the limbic brain from the driver's seat of our neurophysiology. We have to start using the fancy new hardware of the neocortex to develop new pathways that will override the old programming. Then the neocortex can intervene to stop the primitive brain from automatically sending out the chemical signals that cause us to feel and act like cornered animals. Our more evolved brain can begin to run the software that will make the experience of kindness, joy, and peace habitual. This new brain has until recently only been a functioning neurocomputer for saints, scientists, and sages. Yet we can bring its faculties online during our initiation. Indigenous societies that practice meditation, joy, charity, and compassion, all of which are higher brain functions, are far less violent and report experiencing fulfillment and contentment in their lives far more often than those who don't regularly engage in these practices. Functional MRI (magnetic resonance imaging) scans have found that Buddhist monks who've meditated for years have measurable increases in the activity of the prefrontal cortex. In experiments by Andrew Newberg, he describes how when Tibetan monks see a photograph of violence, they respond with the brain centers associated with communion and compassion, unlike the rest of us, who respond with the centers associated with fear or anger.[7] The limbic brain no longer instantaneously takes charge.

If properly brought online through meditation or the practice of the seven virtues, our neocortex will allow us to transcend the fear of death even if we don't believe in an afterlife. It can free us from the demands of the ticking clock and let us experience our connection to all that is and will ever be. The neocortex is programmed for exploration, truth, and scientific innovation, so when we go through an initiation successfully, we activate the neural circuitry that allows us to leave behind superstition, dogma, and hardened religious beliefs and step into a life of discovery. We can finally recognize what a petty, shallow life we've been living in the world of predators and step into the much more nourishing role of creator.

The call to being a creator is a summons to action and service, unfettered by grandiose fantasies about securing one's legacy by saving the world. Once you free yourself from your primitive brain's limited perceptions of what you can accomplish, you discover your greatness. You realize that you're both an immaterial speck and an all-important element in the universe. If you find yourself without a house, you realize that you are a traveler, not a homeless person. If you lose your job, you discover that you are an entrepreneur, not an unemployed person. When your parents pass away, you understand that the earth and the sky are your parents and humanity is your family.

Initiation allows you to experience the pure force of your emotions, unadulterated by memory and divorced from any story. This drains the energy from the neural network, and you are able to replace the negative emotions with higher brain functions. You can establish that the creative neocortical consciousness is the leader of the band. But to do this, you must understand the unique forms of perception associated with each of our four sub-brains, then examine the habits of the prehistoric brain that have given it so much power over you.

Four Levels of Awareness

The reptilian brain, limbic brain, neocortex, and prefrontal cortex are each associated with a particular kind of awareness that developed as these brains evolved. The reptilian brain perceives the physical world without thinking, feeling, analyzing, or trying to find a context for an event. You simply experience it and deal with it. If you twist your ankle when climbing up a mountain path, you hurt, rest for a few minutes, gingerly take a step, and limp forward. Reptilian awareness takes everything literally: a twisted ankle is merely that, not a springboard for feeling sorry for yourself or a metaphor for a difficult journey. Likewise, if you're in battle, you simply crush your opponent's skull and move on to the next adversary before he bashes your head in, feeling no sympathy. The primary mandate of this brain is the drive to survive: *I eat and I kill; therefore I am.* For many thousands of years, reptilian awareness predominated and kept most of humankind building pyramids as laborers and killing others as warriors, and there was little use in seeing the world any other way.

The limbic brain began to establish its authority nearly 200,000 years ago with the discovery of cooking. Our ancestors had been using fires for many years, but at this point in human development we began cooking food regularly. This allowed us to render fiber and proteins more easily digestible, helping us feed our brain, which consumes nearly 25 percent of the fuel we eat. The primary concerns of the limbic brain are feeding, mothering, safety, self-worth, establishing and maintaining the pecking order, and mating: *I hoard and I mate; therefore I am*. Using this brain, we bond with our mothers and search for partners to have sex or parent with. We experience jealousy, betrayal, anger, and resentment. We hoard toys and money. The limbic brain thinks in terms of superstition, religion, morality, and the power of faith. If we look around among our acquaintances, we are sure to find people whose priorities are simply to eat and be comfortable—like a reptile basking in the sun.

Then, nearly 50,000 years ago, our ancestors awakened to the potential of the neocortex, and a sense of aesthetics and beauty emerged. Both the limbic brain and the neocortex appeared as anatomical structures much earlier but did not become a functional neurocomputer until the dates above. These dates are still the subject of intense debate today. Toolmaking suddenly acquired a new level of sophistication after remaining largely unchanged for the previous one million years. And in deep caverns in Southern France and Spain, intricate art began to appear.

In the Upper Paleolithic period, artists and sages braved the dark and the cold to crawl thousands of feet into ancient caves to grace the walls and ceilings with exquisitely drawn images of horses, stags, female forms, and geometric figures. These figures had to be drawn by firelight and must have held mystical significance. The primary drive of neocortical consciousness is to understand how things work and why things happen, giving rise to science, ethics, and philosophy: *I think; therefore I am*.

Around 6,000 years ago, civilization as we know it burst forth in seemingly unconnected areas of the world, as alphabetic writing, mathematics, and city-states transformed the human landscape. Architects designed the great pyramids along the Nile, astronomers in the Yucatán deciphered the movements of the stars and the solstices, and philosophers developed revolutionary ideas along the banks of the Ganges, Sarasvati, Tigris, and Euphrates rivers. A new level of consciousness was attained by a few from among the masses of slaves squaring stones along the shores of the Nile, and these men and women established themselves as the intelligentsia. Language was used to communicate not only the details of the hunt and newfound feelings and emotions but also ideas in the form of written text. The first books of the Bible, the Upanishads, and the *Epic of Gilgamesh* were all written after this time. The drive of this newest brain is to create and to discover. So great was its power that we had to attribute its primary quality to a god, Yahweh: *I AM; therefore I am.*

This level of consciousness is associated with the prefrontal cortex, where you perceive life to be filled with metaphors that help you understand your experiences and put them in a greater context. For example, when you meet up with your friends after your hike, you might tell the story of the twisted ankle as a tale of heroic challenge, a welcome sacrifice to partake of the extraordinary vistas at the mountaintop. While your reptilian brain is completely absorbed by taking the next step, at this level you notice universal elements in that hike. It is no longer a walk; it has become a *journey*, and as such it parallels every great journey undertaken.

Your feelings are likely to shift when you take this perspective. Instead of cursing the person who encouraged you to start up the path, or muttering about the stupid root you tripped over, you recognize that all paths have unexpected twists and turns and obstacles. You know that an experience that yields wisdom or insight is always of value even if it requires a certain amount of effort. In this state, you approach life like a poet, seeing beauty and mystery everywhere and feeling a sense of awe.

This brain helps you lose your sense of separateness as your identity merges with the mountain and the clouds above. The pain in your ankle recedes as you dwell in the beauty of the path. Although the experience of communion may last for only a few moments, its effects last a lifetime and forever alter your perception of yourself and the world. This is the great illumination often associated with initiation. Shamans call it the second awakening, as the first had to do with the awareness that you would die someday.

Distorted Perceptions

One of the reasons it's so hard to change the seven toxic emotions is that we like to think we're rational and logical, that we recognize the difference between fact and fiction, and that we have a firm grasp on the truth. We admit that our reasoning may be somewhat colored by our experiences, but the brain that seeks power, reputation, and security likes to believe we're "too smart" to let our emotions run away with us.

The seven toxic emotions reside as dim sentiments, humming like a computer on sleep mode, ready to jump into action whenever we interpret a neutral situation into one that seems to validate our early life stories. Our mind then scans for facts that fit our narrative, matching them up to the emotions we've just kindled. We bring up a memory of despair and say, "Isn't that always how it is?" The belief that "life is a struggle" was etched into neural networks in our brain long ago. Researchers believe that biological traits, including resistance to disease, may have been etched into the genetic memory banks of our great-grandparents and passed on to us. Researcher Marcus Pembrey noted that the paternal grandsons of Swedish boys who were exposed during childhood to famine in the 19th century were less likely to die of cardiovascular disease.[8] But biological traits are not the only ones to be transmitted transgenerationally. Attitudes, character traits, and beliefs also seem to be passed on from one generation to another, so that the grandchildren of persons who lived during the great depression often feel a greater sense of impoverishment than others. Such negative beliefs spring to life with full force the moment we find evidence to confirm our suspicions—and we always do.

The emotions that stoke our need for power are much stronger than we care to admit. The famous Stanford prison guard experiment of 1971 exposed just how quickly a mentally stable, intelligent person will descend into the brutality familiar to the limbic brain. Designed by the psychologist Philip Zimbardo, Ph.D., the experiment aimed to study how average, psychologically healthy male college students would behave when put in the position of acting as prison guards over their peers. The plan was for the "prisoners" to be held captive in the basement of Stanford University's psychology building. Each participant's role, prisoner or guard, was chosen randomly. Originally, the men were supposed to play their roles for two weeks, but in just six days, the emotional abuse inflicted on the inmates by the guards was so brutal that Zimbardo ended the experiment.

Of course, we'd like to believe that we would be the one prison guard who goes against the grain and acts courageously and heroically, that we would keep our perspective and remain clear-headed. We'd like to believe that had we been conscripted as Nazi prison guards, we would have behaved differently toward inmates of the concentration camps. Perhaps we would have, but evidence shows that human beings very easily give in to the collective pressure to conform.

Emotional trauma to our limbic brain makes us believe that every situation can be told with the simple narrative of bad guys versus good guys, of victims, persecutors, and rescuers. These stories blind us to the truth as we pick and choose facts that support our story and ignore or minimize those that don't. Rather than feel like a weak victim, we choose to play the more satisfying part of either the noble rescuer or the righteous bully. Alternately, we recast our victimhood as a noble martyrdom and use it to try to manipulate others into feeling sorry for us and taking care of us. We do all of this without realizing that we're locking ourselves into a disempowering narrative and a harsh reality.

The "Truths" We Tell Ourselves

The primitive brain confuses the facts with the truth. It twists the evidence to justify our anger, greed, lust, sloth, envy, gluttony, and pride. Understanding the difference between truth and facts allows us to remain vigilant to the distortions of the wounded limbic brain. The stories our ancestors told around the fire were truthful in that they expressed the aspirations and values of the village. Using poetry and imagery, they told ancient lore of heroes and their accomplishments. History and myth were readily blended, and if the facts changed in the retelling, it didn't matter as long as the stories reflected a universal truth that could be recognized by all. Fairy tales are an excellent example of this. The stories of Beauty and the Beast, Cinderella, and King Midas have been told with a hundred variations in countless ages and cultures, all carrying the same messages. Haven't we all known people who tried to help their spouses discover their beauty and stop behaving like beasts?

But as civilization advanced, humans began to equate facts with truth. "Facts," however, can be twisted in many different ways, distorting the truth. We give more weight to one group of facts than another or deny certain facts if they make us uncomfortable. The Catholic Church had no tolerance for Galileo's facts about astronomy, which contradicted its doctrine. Believing that humans are at the center of the universe, with the life-giving heat and light of the sun revolving around us, met the primitive brain's need to validate its self-importance. Believing that we're merely on one of many orbs rotating around the sun and at the mercy of its forces may be the literal truth, but it didn't match up with our longing for a sense of worth, power, and value. The Church and the Pope didn't like this glaring reminder that their god wasn't in charge of the known universe. When the scientific facts didn't match up with our primitive brain's needs, those facts had to be rejected. Even among students of anthropology and mythology, we often look at other religions or worldviews as "myths" but continue to see ours as fact. As you read the sentence above, did your brain hit a bump when you noticed that *god* was not capitalized?

As more people became literate, the storybooks changed from grand myths expressing universal truths to histories composed of facts carefully chosen, assembled, interpreted, and sanctioned by the powerful. Historians and scribes, the new storytellers, wanted to solidify the power of their patrons, promoting the values of their masters. The divine right of kings, the pope as God's representative on earth—these were the kinds of "truths" the powerful sought to communicate through their histories and writings. Humble, ordinary folk and vanquished peoples didn't have a voice in how the narrative was written. Just as the king's official portrait artist took pains to render a jaw more resolute and a face more fair than the king actually possessed, the books that made their way into libraries recorded stories that had been filtered by the powers that owned the printing presses, the paper, and the money to produce tomes that captured the truth as they saw it. It would be a very long time before someone would come up with the idea "Don't believe everything you read."

After literate societies began to carefully construct stories from their hand-picked and sometimes deliberately distorted or invented "facts," people began to believe that "facts" were the same as "truth." They told stories about the neighboring tribe of barbarous cannibals or related "facts" about the old woman at the edge of the village who made potions to heal the ailing, which surely proved she was a witch. The Nazis made up heinous stories portraying Jews as baby snatchers who sacrificed Christian infants, which many Germans believed. The Bush administration offered compelling evidence that Saddam Hussein had weapons of mass destruction that he was ready to use on the West, presenting it as a reason for invading Iraq.

As "facts" came to be seen as evidence of the truth, people began to realize that controlling the facts gave them power. The revolution of Gutenberg's printing press didn't bring about a democracy of facts; it turned the newspapers and, later, television into propaganda machines designed to promote the views of those who owned the media. Inevitably, these individuals were interested in producing good consumers and reducing intelligence to the culturally accepted common denominator. As the anthropologist

Claude Lévi-Strauss said, "The only phenomenon which, always and in all parts of the world, seems to be linked with the appearance of writing . . . is the establishment of hierarchical societies, consisting of masters and slaves, and where one part of the population is made to work for the other part."[9]

Even today, the "truthiness" of a claim often matters more to us than the actual truth because it gives us the illusion of being in the know: if it *feels* true, we decide it must be true. Then we find the facts to support our beliefs so that we can feel brilliant, powerful, or justified. Our limbic brain selectively gathers information from pundits and media outlets that comfort us or feed our pet conspiracy theories by only giving us the facts we agree with. All of this distortion and denial is the result of the brain matching up memory and emotion with facts that fit nicely with its pet theories. The logical neocortex (which is the only brain that knows how to read the newspaper) is enlisted by the primitive brain to validate its fears. The limbic brain gathers facts about how dangerous the world is or how humanity may end in 2012, while overlooking all the evidence for our safety.

As we argue about who has a superior collection of facts, we ignore how carefully we've selected them under the guidance of the four F's— fear, feeding, fighting, and fornicating. We extrapolate from our own experiences and what we've read to prove that we're the ones with the handle on the truth. The next fellow does the same using his group of facts. After it becomes clear that we can't get the other guy to see that we're right and he's wrong, the obvious solution is to whack him over the head and force him to go along with our program. An example of this is the 40-year-old trade embargo of Cuba by the United States, a modern-day siege against a sovereign nation to preserve the U.S. ideological point of view. We reason that we have to burn the village in order to save it.

To undergo initiation, we must stop taking direction exclusively from the limbic brain. We have to forget about embracing "truthiness" and start embracing the truth. We can't do this until we accept responsibility for the beliefs we choose to hold, which can support the deadly emotions of the primitive brain or the enlightening emotions of the higher brain. We can dance with the demons or the angels.

Breaking the Grip of the Limbic Brain and the Stories That Support It

Scientists accept that nothing stays the same for long and that today's best theories belong in tomorrow's trash, and feel secure knowing that they have the ability to tap into their creativity and resilience to find ever-finer descriptions about the workings of the universe. But we stubbornly hang on to the facts as we knew them because the prehistoric brain hates change.

The benefit of a life crisis is that it can kick-start the higher brain so that we can experience authentic breakthrough and transformation. Detached from the wisdom of the neocortex, afraid that we don't have the strength to stand up to our fears, we select and organize facts into a narrative that meets our need to feel that we've got life all figured out, regardless of how unhappy it makes us. It's hard to acknowledge how limiting our beliefs are when we're often rewarded for our strong opinions and seemingly unshakable wisdom. We convince ourselves that we're very clever and then find ourselves stammering in confusion when confronted with facts that contradict all that we know. At that point, we often find a way to integrate these new facts into our underlying ideology, our personal narrative, by bending them and distorting them if we have to in order to make them fit. Take creationism, for example. According to a recent CBS News poll, most people in the United States believe that the dinosaurs and humans walked the earth side by side 6,000 years ago.[10] If you consider the scientific evidence, you have to deny the biblical story of Creation on a literal level, which means you have to call into question all your literal interpretations of Scripture. It's much less unsettling to imagine Adam and Eve frolicking with a T. rex than to start questioning the carefully constructed dogma of religion. We have a tremendous capacity for denial when the stakes are high and we're in danger of losing our pet description of reality.

The Fear-Based Stories of the Lower Self

We cling to the carefully crafted explanations we have for why our lives have unfolded as they have, not realizing that even when they appear to be empowering, they're hindering our growth. One of my students told me that when she was a teenager, she rebelled against her non-nurturing mother by becoming pregnant and went on to become a responsible, good parent whose child was well adjusted and always happy. On the surface, this is an empowering story of triumph, and I'm sure it gives her dignity and pride, but she holds on to it with a death grip. Someday, when her child accuses her of not understanding her, she's likely to deny that her mothering is imperfect, because admitting so would poke holes in her self-created reputation as the "perfect mother" who overcame a bad childhood. Rather than accept that we all "have our moments" and create a genuine sense of security, she invests even more aggressively in her personal narrative.

Another woman I know told me she learned that being a "good mother" doesn't mean being consistent in saying no to your child; it means not being afraid to say, "Well, let's look at the other options." She is parenting creatively, and when she recognizes that she's made a mistake, she tells her children she was wrong and that she's sorry for what she did. Shedding the label of "good mother" frees her up to find creative solutions to parenting challenges instead of trying to maintain an imaginary halo over her head.

A New Relationship to Spirit

When the prefrontal cortex takes its proper place in the holarchy of consciousness, mediating the emotions of our primitive brain, we discover a new relationship to the Divine. We no longer project onto Divinity the role of king, lord, military commander, or punitive father. We let go of the elaborate explanations of the nature of God. The old perceptions of Divinity reflect the limbic brain's reality, in which there are hierarchies of gods, archangels, guardian angels, cherubim, seraphim, saints, popes, archbishops, bishops, priests, and so on, each holding sway over their own sphere of command. The ancient Greeks projected their anxiety about jockeying for position onto their own gods, who had strict rules about who was allowed to reside on Mount Olympus. Their gods and goddesses constantly squabbled over one another's interactions with lower beings such as titans and humans, and treated ordinary men and women like playthings.

Rejecting archaic notions about the Divine, we can interact with Divinity with originality and openness. We aren't afraid that a god with a quiver full of thunderbolts will throw one at us if we don't kowtow to him. We feel no need to bow, scrape, or kiss rings when we engage with Divinity, because we haven't personified the Divine in the likeness of man. We don't see males as the most accurate human representation of God the Father on earth—and therefore, more entitled to power than females.

The new brain allows us to recognize that any of us can become a medicine woman, mystic, or shaman, and we realize that there are no intermediaries between us and the Divine. We understand that we can engage the Divine directly, without shame or fear. The new brain is able to understand this relationship, but the ever-fearful prehistoric brain pulls us back into the clutches of archaic religions founded on fear, sin, and salvation. A different dynamic with the Divine is a tantalizing possibility, but we fear that if we're wrong, we'll be punished for eternity.

Entering the World of Spirit

To escape the predatory world and its fears and longings, we have to be like a serpent and shed our skins. Our personal identity is often tied up in stories of our victories and defeats crafted by the limbic brain. We have to let go of our stories about being a victim of past events and current troubles, as rescuer of those less fortunate (such as our children or spouses, who never seem to appreciate our sacrifices), or as self-righteous persecutor and warrior. We have to discard our belief that power and position have to do with how much we own or the things we accumulate, and be willing to forge an enlightened vision of where we fit in to the larger scheme.

In the world of materialism, we identify with what we own and reduce the loftiest ideas to objects we can possess and control. Freedom is touted as the new BMW we use to cruise the open road. We turn other people into conduits for networking that we can use until the relationship no longer serves us. We identify with our things, not with our essential nature. I travel often to teach and lecture, and sometimes I am asked where I live. I understand that the person is asking me where I keep my things, but I respond that I live *here*. Wherever I am is where I live.

It's difficult to shed the old skin, or identity, because we've grown used to it. It feels like a soft cotton sweatshirt from our college days, and even though it's coming apart at the seams and the iron-on decal has broken into tiny pieces that fall on the floor, we can't bear to let it go. Our way of describing ourselves by the things we own or the work we do or the pain we suffered is so familiar that our closest friends have to bite their tongues every time we repeat the musty stories from the past about our glory days—that horrible ex we finally dumped or the awful thing our brother did seven years ago that made us decide to cut him off for good. Our limbic identity prevents us from having to discover who we are if we're not the adult child of an alcoholic, a divorced mother, or a whistleblower who got forced out of the organization. The primitive brain scoffs at the idea that we can be someone even greater than we've been in the past through any means other than brute force or by acquiring more things. It reminds us of our failures and encourages us to play it safe and ignore the call to be brave and take risks. It can't imagine we can discover the joy of ideas, the beauty of mathematics, the thrill of playing a musical instrument, the enchantment of quantum physics, the delight of life-long learning, and create something even more amazing in our lives than what has gone before.

CHAPTER 4

Archetypal Death and the Great Awakening

There is a hospital bed waiting for me, too.

My grandmother was 82. The resident who had ministered to her was probably 30. So, 25 years from now, when I am in my early fifties, a child will be born who will grow up to become the doctor who will pull the plug on me.

How will I die? What will I die from? Playing with the concept of future life progressions. . . . I see myself dying from a heart condition at an early age. I see myself lying in a hospital bed, surrounded by family members not telling me the truth.

> *Denial.*
> > *Denial.*
> > > *Denial.*

Why?

Death is fearful. We cower from it, and deny it when it comes. But we incubate it within us, like a germ.

Why a heart condition? What is the condition of my heart? Have I ever really opened it up to anyone? Have I ever allowed anyone to come very close? Perhaps I'm setting myself up to die of a heart/love condition. That's it.

Must change that.

Dance of the Four Winds
Alberto Villoldo and Erik Jendresen

We can confront the confusing emotions generated by the primitive brain, and when they arise, we can say, "Here it comes, that old response," and know that it's an automatic reaction to the unknown, to change and unpredictability. Remember that the primitive brain abhors change, while the neocortex delights in it. We can observe our fear and foreboding without believing that they will engulf us or snuff us out. We can feel their power and mystery until they subside, as they inevitably will. We can develop the inner witness, the observer who simply notes what we are experiencing without attaching judgment or a long-drawn-out story to it. This is the secret for accessing higher brain function, short of having our brains rewired after being struck by lightning. This act of witnessing our emotions is the key to meditation and mindfulness practices. The shaman understands that identifying with the observer, rather than with the emotions, is the key to freedom.

The primal fear all adult humans share is the fear of death, which represents the end of the only reality we're aware of. Perhaps it's the awareness of our death, and not the opposable thumb, that makes us distinctly human, for no other creature is aware of its own demise. The fear of death, just like the will to survive, seems to be hardwired into the human brain. Charles Darwin was one of the first to suggest that there is a neurological basis to fear, as most animals—including humans, apes, mice, and birds—respond to fear with the same programmed behaviors, including the release of stress hormones, the experience of paralysis and a startle response, and increased heart rate and respiration.

The problem is that this response is only supposed to be triggered when we're in true danger. The stress of modern-day life, and the perception that disaster is imminent, locks us into a perpetual, low-level fight-or-flight mode. Our sense that the other shoe is about to drop at any moment keeps us operating in a mild state of alert, and we are perpetually on the lookout for real or imagined saber-toothed cats, stockmarket collapses, or malicious bosses. A number of studies document the power of "voodoo death," where the mere suggestion to someone (who believes in voodoo) that they have been hexed results in their becoming gravely ill.

Our fear response is meant to provide a snapshot of danger. Instead, we create an epic movie that engages us long past the point where we should have realized that we're the writer and director, and we're creating a grand tribute to our fear. Sometimes we engage psychologists to help us work through our stories and our feelings about them. Yet talk therapy rarely helps to rewire the neural networks that can allow the higher brain to conduct the orchestra of consciousness.

The Memory/Fear Connection

Our long-term memories of trauma are processed through a region of the brain known as the hippocampus. As we replay our home movie of loss or abandonment, we feel comfort in seeing the familiar images—the Christmas when we were six and Dad's behavior was so upsetting, or the day of our high school senior prom when our date did not show up. All our memories are reinforced, and we forget that other scenes unfolded and were not recorded. Our emotional reality becomes that which we stored in that home movie.

The amygdala is also associated with long-term memory, which explains why fear and pain are such good learning stimuli. When I was a young boy attending a Catholic elementary school, my schoolmates and I were terrified of Sister Mary Immaculata, a stocky, fierce little nun who would strike our knuckles with a ruler whenever we weren't paying attention in class. We nicknamed her El Toro because she would storm into the room like a raging bull and strike at anyone she thought was distracted. Even hearing her heavy footsteps as she strode down the hall gave all of us sweaty palms as we reacted with instinctive dread.

As a child, I didn't know we had the ability to change our fear responses and learn through joy instead of pain. Yet thanks to an evolutionary quantum leap the human brain made about 150,000 years ago, we developed the neocortex, which brought us the possibility of music, poetry, logic, language, and higher-level reasoning, which would take many thousands of years to develop. We no longer needed to feel pain in order to learn. This new brain usurped the amygdala's ancient role in processing emotional memories, but the old brain didn't surrender without a fight. (I still have occasional nightmares of El Toro, who obviously had not discovered the grand capabilities of our new brain.)

The prefrontal cortex provided the hardware for realizing what saints and sages throughout time had discovered: that fear is simply how the lower brain learns to avoid pain, but that joy, discovery, and success are the keys to higher brain function. But we've yet to install the software upgrade that allows us to experience this realization, much as we like to read about it. To install this upgrade, we must undergo initiation to bring the higher brain online.

The Sudden Awakening

Every great awakening occurs swiftly. Jonah is snatched by the whale; Psyche is shocked at the discovery of her lover's beauty; Siddhartha's eyes are opened when he first sees death and illness. Our new biocomputer comes online all at once, in a moment of euphoria, enlightenment, and instant revelation. This awakening must be followed with the great departure and a journey to a new destiny.

The world's religions are replete with stories of this sudden awakening. One of the best known is the tale of the Apostle Paul, a great religious thinker who influenced the development of Christianity. Originally named Saul, he was a Pharisee who had actively persecuted members of the early Christian Church. On the road to Damascus, he had a powerful vision of Jesus, from whom he experienced direct revelation. In the Acts of the Apostles, we learn that "as he neared Damascus on his journey, suddenly a light from heaven flashed around him. He fell to the ground and heard a voice say to him, 'Saul, Saul, why do you persecute me?'" Although Paul never actually met Jesus in person, his sudden awakening inspired writings that became the most influential in the New Testament. The light that knocked Paul off his horse represents his sudden realization. Paul himself writes: "For I want you to know, brothers and sisters, that the gospel that was proclaimed by me is not of human origin; for I did not receive it from a human source, nor was I taught it, but I received it through a revelation of Jesus Christ." Today the phrase "on the road to Damascus" is synonymous with a sudden conversion.

An illumination such as Paul's shakes us up to the possibility of direct knowledge and revelation. But illumination has to be accompanied by an experience of symbolic death and rebirth into a new life. Otherwise it becomes merely another "peak experience" we regale our friends with over a bottle of wine. Soon we return to persecuting those who think differently from us, even as we delight them with stories of our lightning strike. The medicine men and women of old discovered that you could prepare for your initiation, or you could have it happen suddenly and dramatically, as with Paul. The great light of illumination could descend upon you, or your opportunity could come in the more mundane form of a life-threatening illness or accident. Both required you to face your death and discover your courage.

To lessen the terror that arises whenever we become acutely aware of our own mortality, we have developed a marvelous capacity for denial. The denial mechanism is functioning continually. Think about how shaken up you are when you hear a news report about someone who is killed in a freak accident on a road you regularly drive, or who is suddenly diagnosed with a terrible disease and is told there's no cure. The sobering thought, "That could be me!" roils in your mind. You decide not to waste another moment of your precious life, yet the truth is that disaster could befall you any day. Your vow to remember the fragility of life is likely to be forgotten rather quickly.

In fact, the human brain works through denial or inhibition. When you put your shoes on in the morning, you don't want to be reminded all day that you have them on, as that would be distracting. It's only when you step on a tack and feel pain that your awareness goes to your foot. Pain awakens the brain out of denial, so that we feel the impetus to learn. Pain, in fact, is the only way through which the primitive brain learns. Eventually, we become tired of learning through pain and long to learn through joy. Joy, after all, is the best teacher. Even when you're not conscious of your fear of death, you're still experiencing it subconsciously. When I turn on cable news in the morning, I'm subjected to stories of war, economic crisis, tragedy, disease, and suffering that I have little ability to influence. In response, a momentary feeling of dread comes over me; and then I wonder if I ought to limit myself to only one cup of coffee so as not to further stimulate my fight-or-flight response. Chronic low-level stress keeps us unable to listen to our higher brain.

During your initiation, the prefrontal cortex begins to regulate the primitive brain and its fear-based programs. You stop perceiving that you're constantly in a state of threat, and fight-or-flight response resets. The relaxation response will wash over your body, deepening your breathing and slowing your heart rate. You can rest as you realize that the world is a safe place. You can operate from a state of calm instead of a state of terror.

Most systems in the body operate on a *feedback* basis; for example, when you have no more food in your stomach to digest, gastric acid production is turned off. The fight-or-flight response is a *feed-forward* system. The more adrenaline you produce, the greater the amount of brain-damaging cortisol that further increases your adrenaline levels. It's very difficult to reset a feed-forward system; only certain brain foods and meditation practices are able to accomplish this. The initiation process resets this feed-forward system and allows you to discern real from perceived danger. After you complete your initiation, you become fearless like Psyche.

There are two great leaps in awareness that we make during our initiation: the awakening to our mortality, which happens when the neocortex first turns itself on; and the awakening to our immortality, which happens when the prefrontal cortex comes online. If we make the first but not the second, we'll live in constant fear of death. The first intensifies our religious fervor, while the second awakens our audacity and scientific curiosity.

The First Leap: Awakening to Your Mortality

Most likely you first became aware of death when you were a child and your beloved pet died or a person you loved passed away. I remember as a young child going on a trip to a distant city with my grandmother. At the hotel I became distraught and asked her what would happen to me if she suddenly die, as I perceived her as being really old at age 50!

After your initial awareness of death, your limbic brain jumps in to distract you from the painful realization of your own mortality. Intellectually, you know that death is inevitable, yet you've pushed that knowledge to the back of your mind. In our teens and twenties, we understand that death happens, but we think it only strikes other people. We join the military to kill the bad guys, just like in video games, but only in the heat of battle realize that death is very real and can happen to us. A friend who's an insurance agent tells me it's impossible to sell life insurance to anyone under 40, because they just don't believe they'll ever need it. Death and old age haunt everyone after 40. Unless you discover your immortal nature, you'll lose many hours and days worrying about life slipping away.

One of my students, Laura, discovered her mortality when she was 14 and her younger brother was killed by a truck while riding his bike. A few days later, she went to see the new summer movie everyone was talking about, *Jaws,* and watched in shock the famous scene of a boy being attacked by the shark, followed by the eerie image of his mother calling to him in vain from the shore. The strong visuals of the film imprinted the trauma of her brother's loss even more deeply. For years afterward, Laura felt something violent and predatory was following her. She wasn't just afraid to swim in the ocean. She was haunted by dark shadows in her dreams and a sense of being stalked. Her denial mechanism only served to shove these fears into her unconscious mind. It was only after she went through a symbolic death and rebirth during her initiation that she overcame her fears of being hunted by an unseen force. After this initiation, in which she "died" to her old self and was given a new life, she was able to feel safe in the world again.

To forget about our mortality we fuss about our problems endlessly, and we start to fool ourselves that by being thus engaged in the struggles of life, we're outwitting death. Even if our problems cause us suffering, it's nothing compared with the agony we'd feel if we were perpetually aware that the clock is winding down and Death is on its way to claim us. We'd like to believe that Death won't find us when we're constantly on the move and so very busy. Besides, we rationalize, it just wouldn't be fair for Death to come for us when we're making such terrific progress in repairing our flaws.

Another strategy for avoiding death is remaining in a state of pubescent self-absorption. This stage of adolescence is marked by an aggressive denial of one's mortality. A 15-year-old will drink a six-pack of beer and drive a car full of his friends around Devil's Curve at top speed with absolute certainty that the laws of physics are on his side and he won't lose control of the vehicle. When we're stuck in adolescent narcissism, which can extend into our 40s and 50s, we're convinced that we're totally in charge of our lives despite all the evidence to the contrary, and we feel assured of our immortality and importance. We think we're much too valuable to have our identity and all that we've worked for swept away.

After your first brush with death, you understand that you have a limited time here on earth and must use it wisely: making that move or career change you've been postponing, spending quality time with the kids rather than squeezing in another few hours at the office, taking the vacation you've been delaying for years, and apologizing to that person you hurt. You recognize that you're not going to live to be 300 years old, so you don't postpone until tomorrow the joy that you can have today. Reflecting on the actions you've taken—how you've hurt others and been hurt yourself—and searching for life's meaning are noble efforts that originate in this first great awakening. Shamans engage in a process called recapitulation, where they do a comprehensive life review and say goodbye to their history and forgive all who have hurt them in the past. Knowing your vulnerability, you witness yourself and your actions. You are no longer absorbed in your experience and convinced that what's happening to you in this moment is the only important thing on the planet. Really, it's not about you.

This first awakening has to lead to the next step of your initiation, the great departure from your life as you have lived it, and to accepting the tests and challenges of the journey in stage three. Only then will you reach stage four, illumination, and the flowering of a new self and identity, one that has been tempered by life and adversity, and from which you have emerged victorious.

There's a curse associated with becoming aware of one's mortality and getting stuck in the knowledge that this life is finite. We begin to dwell on thoughts of how our life will end and how we're running out of time. The mind starts obsessing over death and the end of our existence and scurries about trying to make it financially before our youth slips away, or finding the right partner before the wrinkles appear. To distract ourselves, we engage in activities designed to stave off death. We get busy, and we accomplish a lot. What we don't do is slow down and become quiet. Silence, meditation, and emptiness would mean staring death in the face, and that makes our primitive fear arise. Afraid of its spell, we quickly dash off to find another distraction.

The shaman knows that the best way to conquer the fear of death is to taste immortality, in the second awakening.

The Second Leap: Awakening to Your Immortality

Identify with your eternal nature—actually experience who you are beyond your ego and your job description—and the fear of death will vanish. To borrow a phrase from Buddhist scholar Robert Thurman, you'll realize that no one gets out of here dead. The shamans of the Amazon believe that anyone who has not experienced the second awakening will, after death, return to the river of souls and lose all individuality. Those who have been initiated will retain their identity even while immersed in that stream. The awakened do not have to carry their wounds with them as karma into their next lifetime.

Recognizing your eternal nature allows you to realize that your true identity won't ever cease to exist, and the part of you that will be shed like an old skin isn't that important anymore. You realize that your worst fear is to waste time by not living fully and to find yourself on your deathbed thinking about all your regrets.

The shaman welcomes the opportunity to gaze into the face of death, whereas most people run away in fear. In many traditions, a seeker would journey to a desolate place—perhaps the high desert or the jungle—to engage in a vision quest. There she would fast and pray, facing and defeating the demons that appeared before her. This was a practice common among the early Christian hermits in the Egyptian desert. These Desert Fathers, as they came to be known, led materially impoverished yet spiritually rich lives. They modeled their spiritual practice after Christ's fasting in the desert for 40 days and John the Baptist's austerities in the wilderness. Eventually, the seeker would symbolically "die" to his earthly existence and awaken to his nature as an infinite being at peace with God.

Such experiences make us aware of our transcendent nature, and can happen during any transcendent experience, such as prayer, making love, or a near-death incident. We have a sudden sense of unity with all that is and ever was, a tremendous sense of awe and humility, and a dissolving of the ego. We die to the way of the flesh and are born to the way of Spirit.

Meditators attain this second awakening as well, and this has been described in Buddhist texts and Patanjali's *Yoga Sutras*, where it is known as *samadhi*, an elevated state of consciousness. The alchemists of the Middle Ages, who supposedly tried to turn base metals into gold and produce an elixir of immortality by chemical means, were actually seeking this spiritual state of illumination, according to Carl Jung's symbolic interpretation of alchemy. The alchemical process was thus a method of purifying the soul, ridding it of all its toxins so that it could shine brilliantly. The alchemists understood that once a person is awakened to his undying nature, experiencing it instead of just believing in it, he never loses it. Once the spell of death is broken, one is forever changed. Having found the fountain of youth, one is free of the fear of death that stalks others.

Those who are quite aware of their mortality but not of their immortality get stuck in a terribly uncomfortable no-man's-land. If you haven't experienced the second awakening, it can be hard to conceive of this other reality. Consider that to a fish in a pond, water is so enveloping that it's not part of his awareness. Recognizing the water's existence would require him to be transported above the pond to a spot from which he could gaze down at his body gently swimming through the reeds and see all that surrounds him. In his little pond, there is only his limited reality. Like the poet Kabir exclaimed, "I laugh when I hear that the fish in the water is thirsty."

We, too, live in our little pond until we've gone through the second awakening. We then observe and experience the universe as being inseparable from ourselves, and we understand our place in creation.

The Archetypal Death

The second awakening involves an archetypal death and resurrection that can be just as frightening as physical death. We want to believe we won't lose everything someday—our sense of ourselves, our attachments to the people we love, and all that we've ever worked to achieve, from our success to our skills to our growing comfort in our own identity. We don't want to shed that skin, which provides so much security, unless there's a guarantee that we can hold on to what really matters to us. We remain unconvinced that what lies on the other side will be at least as good as what we've got now, if not better.

During each initiation we experience the death of a grand myth about ourselves. One of my friends, for example, is in love with love. He meets a woman, sleeps with her that night, and a week into his torrid affair, he is utterly convinced she is "the one." The infatuation lasts a couple of months or so, until he finds the next true love. What he's really in love with is the image of himself as the grand lover. He's in denial of his inability to complete the initiation into the role of the lover who genuinely surrenders himself to create a union of two people. Instead, he is standing in the doorway admiring his fantasy self, unable to step across the threshold to truly unite with a partner.

We resist the archetypal death because, however painful the circumstances of our lives may be, we take comfort in their familiarity. But if we were to die to who we are and lose all that's familiar, what would become of us? Our identity seems extremely important to us. After all, having a sense of self is part of what defines us as human. The chimp in the tree isn't thinking, "I could use a stick as a tool to get the ants out of that anthill, but that's not really my personal style, and what if the other chimps thought I was acting strange?" Even the male gorilla who is fighting another for dominance over the females in their group isn't thinking about what he has to do to earn his place as the fiercest, strongest ape on the mountain, and whether his mother will be proud of him. When the time is appropriate, he beats his chest to communicate to another male to beware of his strength and back off. We, in contrast, spend an enormous amount of time worrying about who we are and what our place is within the community.

There's nothing wrong with being proud of what you've accomplished or happy with who you are at this stage of life, but whatever your identity and reputation, it's not all that you are. It's not even the most important part of who you are. Your life, like everyone's, is going to change again and again over time. You'll go through the various stages of life and age until you get to the point where you shed your body and the person known as you no longer exists on earth. If you've experienced your immortality, if you've felt the tranquility and joy of stepping beyond your personality, beyond time, the loss of your identity ceases to matter so much to you.

Our soul knows that there are times when we have to let go of all we know, all we feel, and all that our senses tell us, and take a leap of faith into a dark, unknown abyss, trusting that we'll emerge safely. We know that this is the case with love and intimacy. But that is the price for all real growth in our lives. If we try to settle for merely patching the old skin in the vain hope that it will last us forever, we're just postponing the inevitable. We don't go from chrysalis to butterfly: we spend our lives dreaming butterfly dreams while crawling to the next leaf.

The shaman knows he must master the art of dying and being resurrected so that he can undergo the archetypal or sacred death again and again, creating a new life for himself when the writing on the wall says, "It's time to let go of the old." He's able to change with grace, embrace the new, and live a truly creative life no matter what his age or circumstances. He's able to let go of the narrow definitions of lover, parent, and sage, and approach these stages innovatively.

The Spanish mystic Saint John of the Cross described the archetypal death as "the dark night of the soul," which he saw as a necessary trial in spiritual life. It's the longest night we can possibly imagine, because there are no clocks to orient us and reassure us that dawn is approaching. We can't see what's up ahead, yet we have to give ourselves over to the process, letting go of control and our sense of who we are. It's in our nature to endure this night, not with faith and prayer, but with panic and frantic clawing about for a light switch—and a mirror, to make sure we still are who we think we are. If we can accept that we'll probably enter the abyss kicking, screaming, cursing, and wishing we could magically be transported back in time to the moment before we took our fall, we'll move more quickly from resisting this change to working with it and discovering what it has to offer us. This at least is how it has always worked in my life. I know enough about the journey now to let go with a giant scream and a smile on my face.

Lifting the Luminous Energy Field

The Pharaohs of ancient Egypt had their burial sarcophagi carved out of stone and the prayers for the soul's safe passage beyond death inscribed in them long before they needed to use them. In fact, carving a sarcophagus took a very long time by the hands of skilled stonemasons and priests. The king was carefully measured for size and actually had a chance to undergo his second awakening after the royal coffin was finished. He ceremonially lay in his deathbed as the heavy lid of the coffin was lowered into place. The priests who had designed the sarcophagus knew exactly how much air remained inside and how long one could remain alive in a state of deep meditation after consciously lowering the heart rate and oxygen consumption. During this initiation, the king was expected to leave his physical body and journey to the dark region of space beyond the stars, where he would be instructed in the arts of enlightened rulership. He would return just as the air was running out and the top was being lifted, infused with a wisdom he would bring to his kingdom.

Shamans learned to engage a similar practice without the need of building a sarcophagus, by momentarily disengaging the luminous energy field from the physical body. They call this practice the Spirit Flight. The luminous energy field is what ancient Egyptians called the Ka, or life force. It is the aura, the field of light that envelops and informs the physical body. During this practice the shaman was able to leave his body and journey to the celestial realms to learn the arts of enlightened living. She did so by disengaging each one of her seven chakras. The chakras are energy centers in the body that are shaped like funnels, the wide mouth extending an inch or two outside our body, and the narrow tip connecting to our brain and spinal cord. This practice was traditionally performed with the help of another, but you can do it for yourself.

EXERCISE: Spirit Flight

Set your intention to journey to the heavenly realms, where you can receive instruction and healing. Lying comfortably on your bed, feel with your right hand for your *first chakra*, above your pubic bone. Try to sense its swirling vortex of energy. Then spin it carefully three to four times in a counterclockwise direction, as if your body were the face of the clock and your hand the hand of the clock. Take a few deep breaths and proceed to:

The *second chakra*, two fingers bellow your belly button. Sense its swirling vortex of energy. Then spin it carefully three to four times in a counterclockwise direction. Take a few deep breaths and proceed to:

The *third chakra*, at your solar plexus at the center of your chest. Sense its swirling vortex of energy. Then spin it carefully three to four times in a counterclockwise direction. Take a few deep breaths and proceed to:

The *fourth chakra*, at your heart. Sense its swirling vortex of energy. Then spin it carefully three to four times in a counterclockwise direction. Take a few deep breaths and proceed to:

The *fifth chakra*, at the base of your throat: Sense its swirling vortex of energy. Then spin it carefully three to four times in a counterclockwise direction. Take a few deep breaths and proceed to:

The *sixth chakra*, at your forehead. Sense its swirling vortex of energy. Then spin it carefully three to four times in a counterclockwise direction. Take a few deep breaths and proceed to:

The *seventh chakra*, at the top of your head. Sense its swirling vortex of energy. Then spin it carefully three to four times in a counterclockwise direction. Take a few deep breaths.

Notice the sensations you have and any images that appear to you.

Shamans do this practice after fasting and meditation. If your mind is full with the activities of your day, it will be more difficult to experience this journey to the upper world. But if you can still your mind enough, after a number of attempts you will notice that you are able to rise above your body, and perhaps see it below you, and meet luminous beings and spiritual teachers who instruct you in the art of life.

Resisting Initiation

Refusing to enter the dark passage of initiation will drain us and throw us into crisis. Whenever we resist change, our frantic flailing about and anxious thoughts will prevent us from using our energy in a productive way. The prospect of a new identity is both enticing and frightening, so we sometimes put great effort into holding on to the old ones with the proverbial "death grip." We may try to figure out how we can use our anger to bully the universe into behaving itself. Or we may feel so overwhelmed by our losses that we become paralyzed and depressed. We start to perceive life as a futile struggle. We are in crisis.

Being busy all the time may distract you from the little voice inside that whispers that transformation is inevitable. Sometimes you're tempted to settle for mere reinvention. You might take on a new lover, move to a different division of the company, relocate to a new city, go on a revolutionary new diet, and so forth. Some of my students have confided that their lives seemed to be chugging along until one day they were shocked to receive a life-threatening diagnosis. Their ability to stifle that little voice was so powerful that it had to find another way to get their attention. I try to help them see the illness as a big whack upside the head from the universe, which has been nudging them to let go of their resistance and the belief that their earthly identity is the sum of who they are.

Curing a disease doesn't necessarily heal the soul. However, allowing the soul to travel forward into the next stage of growth often results in the body's healing itself. Our energy system is freed up to use its stores of power to right what has gone wrong at a cellular level. Cancer is just one example of a disease that can be a call to initiation. The natural renewal mechanism that's programmed into every cell, known as apoptosis, is shut off in cancer cells. A tumor doesn't recognize that it has to stop busily dividing and reproducing and allow its cells to die. It insists on achieving temporal immortality at the cost of disease. I have seen clients start to heal when they surrender to initiation and taste their immortality. Their body is able to reset itself to natural rhythms, and the healthy cycle of cells can return. They're able to heal at a deep level, and inform the physical body that its cells don't need to wage a war of survival in a futile attempt to stave off death. Curiously, cancer is a great example of the breakdown of a holarchy, where the needs of the cell are put ahead of the needs of the organism.

The Relationship between Death and New Life

All deaths, all endings, are a passage to the next beginning. The first law of thermodynamics states that energy can be changed from one form to another, but it can neither be created nor destroyed. As energy beings, we shed our bodies and let them become part of the cycle of life in the physical world while our essential self moves forward into the next state of being. A Lakota medicine man once told me that when the ancestors die, they're buried and return to the earth to form part of the trees and all of nature, reassimilated into the greater whole. For a long time I thought this meant that their bodies became fertilizer, mulched into food for trees and flowers, but later I understood that their consciousness endured and became part of the whole of Creation once again. And after you had mastered the second awakening, there was someone left to experience this ecstatic and terrifying merging.

Once we understand that all death is merely a transition into a different form of life, change ceases to be so frightening. We can take comfort in knowing that we'll be resurrected, even if we have no clue what our new existence will be like. Thinking about life and death as a cycle is not new; many ancient cultures had symbols and ceremonies marking the connection between the old and the new, the dead and the living. Folk culture gives us the image of Death as the Grim Reaper, a faceless being in a hooded black robe who carries a sharpened sickle and points his bony finger at his latest victim, designating that this poor soul must come along with him to the unknown world of the dead. But the sickle he carries is a tool of the harvest, used to cut the grain away from the stalk so that it can be made into bread to feed and sustain life. If we leave the grain on the stalk, it will grow mold and become useless. Without death, without the harvest, there can be no life. The Grim Reaper is derived from the Greek god Cronus, who fathers the goddess Aphrodite. Like the stalk of wheat that contains within it the seeds of future harvests, we also contain within us the "seeds" of our future life, which are discovered during initiation. This discovery allows us to shed the fear of death that haunts humanity.

Going into Free Fall

Archetypal death is not literal, even though it sometimes feels as if we are physically dying. This symbolic death, which is part of every initiation process, is a free fall into that abyss of the unknown. It includes a death of old ideas, of limiting beliefs that are no longer work for us, of old friendships that were never right, even of old habits such as how we dress and how we present ourselves. As the prelude to a new mythic journey, archetypal death requires abandoning the old maps that once helped us to navigate our lives. There is a story of a hiker who comes across a man at the foot of a mountain with a wooden raft strapped onto his back. The hiker asks him why he is carrying a raft, as there are no rivers or lakes on that mountain, and the man responds that the raft saved his life once when he was near the sea. This raft represents all the beliefs and skills that once served us but that have become a burden that we carry on our backs.

When you finally accept that the person you once were no

longer exists, you may wonder, "Why did it all have to end?" For many years, I identified with the image of the young, daring explorer who went off into the Amazon. The *New York Times* even published a review of one of my books and titled it "Indiana Jones Blows His Mind." Most of my clothing was made by North Face and Patagonia. Then, when I turned 50, I noticed how my hair was graying, how I still enjoyed the Amazon but only from a comfortable lodge, and how ridiculous it was for a man my age to carry on like a young explorer. Then, to top it all off, my son began calling me "old man." For a time I was angry and frustrated. I understood that people grow old, but I didn't expect it to happen to me. I had all the wind taken out of my sails. Then I decided to embark on my initiation. I knew I had to let the young explorer die, and grow into the sage. I cried at the loss of my youth and was terrified at the prospect of old age. Yet I knew I had to start mentoring younger men and women, and not feeling threatened or that I had to compete against them. And I knew I needed a new wardrobe.

In our culture, women learn that it's okay to cry, whereas men are socialized to avoid it at all costs. The women I know claim that a "good cry" is cathartic. It's hard for men to imagine that a cry could ever be good, but women understand something men don't: letting out our feelings lightens us, allowing us to return to a higher brain state and create joy again. The sense of being unburdened starts to rise inside us and peak as the crying subsides. Crying is the way the limbic brain heals. Laughter is the medicine of the neocortex.

A good cry happens when you simply experience your feelings without all the stories associated with them. When I was going through my initiation into sagehood, I cried many times as tears welled up on their own. I did not cry because I was sad—I was sad because I cried. Then the tears, and the sadness, washed through me.

Once you stop feeling that the world's conspiring against you, you'll recognize that your story of loss and resurrection is an archetypal human experience that we all share. You'll see it's a story that offers the opportunity for redemption, growth, and enlightenment.

Being Reborn as a Creator

Once you experience the feelings that surface when you realize that an aspect of your life is ending, you can find a certain perfection to your life right now and see it as the clay of creation. What possibilities lie in that ball of clay?

My initiation into sagehood was not smooth and easy. It took many months of struggle, anger, and disappointment. I felt that my masculinity was at stake, that women would begin looking at me with kindness instead of attraction, that young men would no longer be awed or impressed by who I was, but instead would pity me. That year, I traveled to Africa and saw how the old wildebeests were ousted from the herd by the virile young ones, and how they gazed forlornly at their lost companions from the distant hilltops. That year, everywhere I went and everything I did mirrored my misery. After the Africa trip, I told my editor that I had nothing more to say and was done writing books.

On the brink of initiation, you'll be aware that what you're experiencing is not simply death or an ending. You'll see that it's a process of creation in which you are a full participant. Yes, the universe has its own ideas about what comes next, but you are a co-creator of your new life and your new identity. You'll recognize some aspects that haven't changed—maybe it's your sense of humor or your exuberance—but you'll realize these don't define you or limit you. If you've always been a leader, you'll be able to acknowledge the part of you that's a natural follower or supporter of others. If you've always been the nurturer in relationships, you'll discover the self that can receive, that allows others to experience being the giver. The following year, after I completed that initiation, I called my editor back and told her I was working on a new book. I realized that while indeed I had written everything I had to say as an explorer and anthropologist, I was just beginning to discover my authorship as a sage.

When a monk enters a monastery, his head is shaved, his street clothes are exchanged for a simple robe, and he receives a new name. Stripped of his identity, the initiate is free to discover who he is becoming. As part of your own initiations, you, too, will have to let go of the outer garments of who you were. This doesn't mean that you go and shave your head, but simply that you drop the façade and relax a bit the finely crafted face that you put on in the morning. Then, and only then, can you discover who else is behind the eyes that look back at you from the mirror.

CHAPTER 5

The Stages of Initiation

I wanted to catch him, but the midwife would have none of it. I did get to see his head coming out of his mother's birth canal, and the final contractions, after which my son entered this world. He even seemed to have a smile on his face, but the midwife later explained to me that it was my imagination. My job had been to videotape the birth, and holding the camera gave me something to do and got me out of the way. But when his little head came out, I was too overcome with joy and forgot all about the filming.

The panic did not hit until I got to hold his squirming little body a little bit later. "What am I going to do with this creature that can't eat, walk, or talk?" That's when the thought crossed my mind that I could just go back to the Amazon and carry on with my research. I had become knowledgeable of the rainforest and its ways, but knew nothing about being a father. I knew I could get into the jungle and out again safely. But would I survive parenting?

Soon, I decided to take a year off from work and allow my son to teach me to become a father. From explorer to dad. What a leap!

Journal

In early spring, when the child was born, an eagle flew high over the tepee. As the boy grew up, the eagle always followed him as he hiked through the mountains, circling above him. One night in a dream he met the eagle by a waterfall. The following morning he hiked to the waterfall and hid behind the torrent of water, from where he spied the eagle eating a salmon on a rock. As he stepped out from his hiding place, the eagle hopped over to him and offered him the fish. With time the eagle and the boy became friends, and when he became a man he fell in love with the great bird.

One day he climbed high up a cliff to where the eagle had her down-filled nest, and he professed his love for her. She explained that she had watched over him since he was born, and that they could live together as eagles do, but then he could never return to his people or their ways.

Every day the boy climbed down for his water and corn, and brought it up the steep walls. One day he was very late, and when he returned he told the eagle that he must go back to his people, for they were about to be attacked by a fierce neighboring tribe. She reminded him that he had promised never to go back to the ways of humans and their wars, but the young man defied her. That evening the eagle flew over the camp and observed a maiden as she applied war paint to the young man, a tear running down the eagle's cheek. The next morning she saw the warriors on their horses advancing toward one another on the open field.

In the dust and chaos of the battle, she saw an enemy throw his spear at her beloved. The eagle swooped down from the sky and took him in her talons before the lance struck his heart. As she carried him above the clouds, he said that he knew she would save him. Flying high above the mountains, she cried, and explained that what is destined cannot be changed, and released him—for it is better that death come to you from your beloved than your enemies' hand

This tale, a traditional teaching story from the Great Plains, shows that once you make your vows of love, you may never go back to your old ways. The price you pay for doing so is death— whether the loss of your life or of a relationship you were not fully ready to commit to. In every great initiation, we have to leave the old ways behind. If we want to fly peacefully with eagles, we must reject forever the ways of war.

In traditional societies, life passages are seen as opportunities for initiation. Puberty, marriage, and parenting all required the initiate to let go of an identity that had become important to him or her. Rituals marking such passages were solemn, a sign of the intensity of emotional upheaval the initiate had to undergo, and the importance of the new identity to the rest of the community. In today's secular society, however, such rites of passage are commercialized and even trivialized. High-society cotillions, extravagant bar mitzvahs, grandiose wedding ceremonies—and the inevitable retirement cruise—can get in the way of fully understanding what it means to let go of one stage and embrace a new one. Amid the jubilant celebration, we often forget that growth requires sacrifice.

Initiation allows us to acknowledge the gravity of our loss. The old self shrivels up and peels away, and with it goes a chapter of our lives. Initiation allows us to walk through the door in our new skin. It helps us to make the transition deep in our soul, so that we don't find ourselves being stalked by our lost opportunities or our biological clock. The woman in perimenopause who can't reconcile her missed chance for motherhood is now able to let go of the dream of being a literal mother and discover other ways she might perform mothering. The man who can't let go of his image as the young, handsome, conquering warrior is able to complete the initiation of marriage. Otherwise, he'll remain unable to surrender in partnership with a woman and unable to attract a woman who is interested in him, not his money and power.

If you haven't already achieved the first awakening by midlife, you will face a loss so profound that it causes you to question all you know and all you are. You'll wake up one morning and ask: What have I become? Who is this person sleeping next to me? Such a crisis is deeply disorienting. If you can engage this crisis in a ritual manner, you may be able to avoid confronting it at the level of physical reality. You won't have to get the dire diagnosis from your doctor, or end up in a car crash, or be devastated when your parents' health fails and their care falls entirely on your shoulders. A monumental crisis will automatically rearrange your priorities. When faced with such a challenge, you must quench the fires, but between breaths you have to ask yourself: What is it that is dying? What is it that is being born? What have I missed in my life? Was I welcomed into the world wholeheartedly? Did I go through my initiation to become a man or a woman? Did I surrender to my partnership or marriage? If you answer these questions truthfully, your ambivalence and self-justifications will disappear. Then you'll find yourself at the stage of the awakening, ready to embark on your initiation and choosing to live according to what matters most to you.

The Four Stages of Initiation

Humans have always found ways to ritualize the process of initiation to prevent our emotions from overwhelming us. A ritualized death, such as one experiences through the Spirit Flight practice, as well as surrendering to the intensity of our fear, anger, or hopelessness, provides us with the security of knowing that when life tests us, we'll pass. The Spirit Flight is an energetic process that you do in the privacy of your home. The shaman knows, however, that in a full-blown initiation, the sense of loss is quite real. Jonah must have been convinced he would never make it out the belly of the beast. Going through the rites in your urban sweat lodge makes for a beautiful ceremony and actually prepares you for the real thing. On the other hand, while a weekend drumming workshop with the guys can be a bonding experience, remember that your true initiation waits for you at home with your loved ones.

All initiations require that you undergo a four-stage process:

- The awakening
- The great departure
- The tests
- Illumination

Understanding these stages will help you map where you are in your journey of transformation and prepare yourself for what comes next.

The Awakening

At the beginning of any great change, you're at the stage of the awakening, still thinking of yourself as an adolescent and not an adult, or as a single person and not a spouse, or a paragon of health and not a patient with an illness. And then something happens that shakes up your world; your eyes open, and nothing is ever the same again. You put away the toys of childhood. You are no longer available for a boxing match with your partner. The realization strikes like a lightning bolt. Yet you continue to cling to who you were, fearful of what will become of you if you shed the skin that has served you so well. In fact, advertisers seize on our insecurities during this stage to try to convince us that if we buy a particular automobile, we'll be able to remain vibrant, youthful, independent, and sexy, even though we're using it for utilitarian purposes. And if we buy the right computer, we will produce brilliant books. Much of our gross domestic product is generated by businesses—from plastic surgery clinics to motorcycle manufacturers to the wedding industrial complex—profiting from our ambivalence, confusion, and trepidation during this stage of the awakening.

The Great Departure

In the great departure, you realize that the old skin is no longer worth keeping, and like Siddhartha you decide to leave the palace, renounce the riches, and ditch the royal attendants. If you don't take this step consciously, you are dragged into it kicking and screaming, as Jonah was. You're stripped to your essential self, and the things that mattered to you—the status, the job, the car, the spouse, the house—are taken away from you, literally or metaphorically. It may be that you do not lose your spouse, but your marriage will cease to make sense. You may still have your house, but it will no longer feel like home.

However, if you take this step consciously, you realize that you are not your cancer, that you are not your divorce, and that you are not a freewheeling adolescent in your 30s anymore, thank God! The alchemists called this stage *nigredo*, the blackening, burning, and breaking down of the old structures until you reach a point where you can no longer discern what is real in your life and what isn't. Jung considered the *nigredo* an essential stage for individuation, the process of becoming a whole person. It's the point at which you struggle with the pain of your loss, lamenting, "If only I'd married the other one . . . if only I hadn't dropped out of school . . . if only it had all been different."

In the great departure, you leave the job, the marriage, or the house. You begin to accept that you can no longer live as who you were. As you move through this stage, you metaphorically toss away the old set of clothes and don sackcloth, the robes of a monk—for a while, at least, before you go out and buy a new wardrobe. You explore a new set of habits and beliefs, and invest in literal representations of the new you that is still to be revealed. Sometimes at this point in a transition, we adopt an almost religious zeal for our new role and an unrelenting disdain for the old. We'll preach to our old drinking buddies about how wonderful it is to be sober, lecture our single friends on how fantastic it is to be married, and insist to our childless friends that they can't possibly imagine how wonderful it is to be a parent. Although we've let go of our former sense of who we are, it takes a while to feel comfortable with the new, and often there's a lingering fear that maybe this stage isn't so great after all. In fact, if you look back at old pictures, you may cringe at the images of yourself aggressively adopting a new identity that really wasn't you. The clothing of the swinging bachelor or the completely contented suburban mother didn't quite fit, but you donned it anyway in the hope that the off-the-rack role someone else dreamed up would somehow end up fitting you perfectly.

When you don't complete the process of the great departure, you get stuck in your shadow. The unhealed parts of yourself begin to dominate your life. You are seduced into defining yourself by what you are not instead of discovering what you might become. You think, "I'm not rich enough, smart enough, or strong enough to get out of my predicament." The result is terminal boredom. Your unending search for your true self and unique identity bores everyone, including you. Man is the only animal capable of ennui, and that's exactly what we experience when we fail to complete this stage in the transition.

When Moses led the Israelites out of Egypt, he first had to remind them that they were not born to be slaves; they were God's chosen people. This was their awakening. Afterward he had to convince the ones who would listen that they should brave the ruthless desert for as long as it took to find their promised land. The departure from Egypt was not easy; soon the Israelites were being pursued by the Pharaoh's armies and found that the Red Sea blocked their escape. Then the famous miracle described in the Book of Exodus occurred: the Red Sea parted, allowing the Israelites to escape. But according to Jewish legend, the waters did not part until the Israelites were nose deep in the water. And this was only the beginning. Many more challenges and tests of faith were to come during the 40 years of wandering in the desert.

A strong will and determination are needed to enter this stage, yet they aren't enough to propel you forward. People can spend years caught in this stage of the great departure, leaving one job or relationship after the next, and going from one self-help workshop to another, without entering the next stage, the tests.

The Tests

Immediately after your departure, you enter the stage of the tests, in which you will unearth your emotions and banish your demons. Once they were no longer slaves, the Israelites became homeless wanderers, squatters gathered around an oasis. Just when you think you made it over the bridge to the other side, you realize that a list of fearsome tasks awaits you—each of which will invite you to banish one of the seven toxic emotions. The alchemists called this stage *albedo*, the whitening stage, in which your facets are ground away and polished, and you are purified.

In this stage of purification, the full cacophony of emotions rises to the surface. All the demons are let loose from their cages, we are tempted to become angry at ourselves and others, lust after what we feel would make us happy, and become slothful. But during this stage we also begin to think of ourselves as travelers on a quest. Even if we do not know where we are or where we are headed, we trust that we will be guided.

When a tree dies, its leaves and trunk fall to the ground and disintegrate, eventually becoming food for a new plant. In the stage of the tests, you mulch the old roles, identities, beliefs, and behaviors into the soil from which your new life will spring. Psyche is no longer a forlorn wife but a woman on a mission. You let go of any concerns about being inadequate, and you fearlessly acknowledge that you may not be fully prepared to step into your new life, but you are absolutely ready for it. In the stage of the tests, you no longer say, "I am not my cancer." You're able to discover how your cancer saved your life by serving as a wake-up call. Jung compared this stage to the alchemical process of turning silver into gold—*citrinitas*, or "yellowing." Silver was thought of as a lunar element and thus was able to shine only by reflecting the light of the sun. In contrast, gold was seen as a solar element shining with its own light. During the tests, the soul shines with its own light, even in the midst of adversity. Jung associated this stage with the discovery of the Wise Old Man or Wise Old Woman archetype within, which represents our own internal source of wisdom and knowledge.

During the tests, you are called to action. You have to embark on the epic journey, face the monsters and demons that lurk deep inside you, and either come back victorious or not at all.

Illumination

In the fourth stage, illumination, you resurrect after dying to all the limitations of an old identity. Known in the alchemical work as the *rubedo*, or reddening, it's the stage in which you accept who you have been in the past, and are able to acknowledge that you've learned. At this stage, you're open to all that you might be and become a mystery unto yourself. Like an actor who refuses to be typecast, you're willing to reappear in a new form, gliding easily from dark drama to light romantic comedy. Once, while hiking in Canyon de Chelly in Arizona, I met a Navajo medicine woman. When I asked her name, she replied, "The red-rock canyon walls am I, the desert wind am I, that child who did not eat today at the reservation am I."

Jung referred to this stage as the individuated self, a state of wholeness in which you are no longer identified with or defined by the sum of your parts. You are no longer the effect of an earlier cause, the outcome of that crushed teen romance that impacted the rest of your relationships. You can't be defined by anything in your history. Not even the genes you inherited from your parents define you exclusively anymore; who you are becoming can even transform your physiology now. The shaman believes that at this stage we can even grow new bodies that are free of their genetic inheritances, and that can age, heal, and die differently.

But for this stage to be authentic, we must come back with boons for others. This stage cannot be only about *me*. The Buddha came back from his quest with the Four Noble Truths. Jesus came back from the desert and taught humanity to turn the other cheek and practice peace. Psyche returned from the underworld with the gift of inner beauty for all women. Gandhi practiced nonviolence even when assaulted by English soldiers, and became a symbol of freedom for the world. If we come back from this last stage merely with another bit of insight about our lives, it has not been an authentic initiation. This does not mean preaching to everyone your great discoveries or believing you must write a book about your perilous journey. The urge to tell everyone is a sure indication that you are stuck in the stage of the great departure. After illumination you have no need to convince anyone of anything, yet you will share gladly when asked.

The gift of illumination is the second awakening, the realization of your undying self.

The Inevitability of Transitions

Change happens more rapidly now than it ever did in the past. One hundred years ago, you were trained for a job that you worked at for your entire life. Today, the average American will have more than three different careers over the course of his or her life. Our need for successful endings and initiations arises more often than it did in agricultural societies. We even go through some initiations more than once, as we change professions in midlife, find new romantic partners, or resettle our household across country. College students are training for jobs that didn't exist when they graduated from high school. People marry two, three, and four times, often becoming parents to a new set of stepchildren. Yet we're less likely today to recognize how crucial the initiatory process is to help us embrace our loss and brave the unknown.

We've subscribed to a vision of perpetual youth that promises we can enjoy the benefits of being a child and the privileges of adulthood while avoiding any responsibilities. It takes courage to leave behind the wounded child and maintain faith that we'll find happiness in the next stage of life. When we try to put on the brakes by experiencing our passages only at the level of hormones and wrinkles, or by means of contrived or overly planned rituals, we mimic—but forestall—the deep shift that can occur. A wedding is a celebration of a union, but also a death to a single life that centered only around you. It is a time of both joy and mourning. In medieval Europe, a wedding was more like a funeral than a celebration for the bride, as she would now have to submit to the will of her husband, who became her master and sole source of support. Or she was married to a former adversary in a brokered arrangement to secure peace and obtain allies. Love and marriage, in fact, have only been equated with each other since the early part of the 20th century. Now, in the 21st century, Western societies are exploring things we never imagined possible, such as same-sex marriage. Instead of wrestling with the old image of yourself as a lone traveler who answers to no one and forcing yourself to remain faithful to your spouse, you can design a new type of relationship where you are not wearing a ball and chain. You can craft a union where you do not lose your liberty or identity, and you do not have to enter into physical or emotional servitude.

To succeed in your initiation, you have to surrender to the swirl of bewildering feelings that arise, and experience them devoid of any sentimental or dramatic story, until you transcend them at last. During a funeral, you allow yourself to feel both grief and joy: for example, you are devastated at the loss of your mother, glad that she is no longer suffering, and secretly relieved that the burden of taking care of her has ended. During a wedding, you may feel sad and happy, confused and shocked. The mix of emotions is part of the process and can't be avoided. As the witty writer Gore Vidal put it, "Whenever a friend succeeds, a little something in me dies." There is no correct way to parent, to partner, to handle a fatal diagnosis, or to come out as a lesbian. You can only rewrite the role after experiencing the terror of the loss and the bewildering feelings that accompany it. When you do that, the process will feel organic and natural.

Water and fire are natural elements that have been used for millennia to craft simple yet authentic rites of initiation. These elements also allow us to purify our feelings and wash away regrets about the old so that we may welcome the new. You may want to use them as you craft your initiation.

Water, Fire, and the Flow of Timelessness

Water, a symbol of purity and rebirth, is a familiar ingredient of religious rituals all over the world. In Christian baptism, water ritually cleanses a person of the sins of his ancestors and prepares him to enter his new spiritual life. Among Orthodox Jews, the mikvah is a ritual immersion in water that marks the end of a wife's monthly period and the beginning of renewed intimacy in her marriage; men also purify themselves in a mikvah on special occasions. Hindus wash away the old and commit to a new course by immersing themselves in the sacred Ganges River. Cathedrals in Europe were often built on top of pagan wells, which were considered holy sites of great power, where people not only came for the life-giving qualities of water but to be spiritually cleansed and healed. And the healing waters at the Roman Catholic shrine of Lourdes, France, continue to draw thousands of pilgrims annually.

Maybe on a subconscious level, we use water in ritual because we're recalling our emergence from the sea in that evolutionary moment when we became land creatures and let go of our lives in the primordial ocean. Or perhaps we intuitively recognize that water ushers us into the world, preceding our journey through the birth canal. In some traditions, water is the element associated with the archetypal Mother, who gives birth to the new. Agricultural societies, because of their dependence on water for farming, typically use water for initiations.

We have seen that water symbolizes purification and rebirth, but water also has another important meaning for the shaman: it represents the river of timelessness. In the shamanic world view, time moves in all directions—it rushes downstream, collects in pools, and even seems to travel back to its source in deep tides. The past doesn't necessarily determine the future, and the future may influence the present.

A shaman is able to enter the flow of this invisible river when in a heightened state of awareness induced by fasting, meditation, or plant substances. Within the river of timelessness he learns that endings are also beginnings—that there is life in death and death in life, and that neither the chicken nor the egg came first. He lets go of his fear of death and allows himself to be carried through eddies and over slippery rocks in what sometimes seems to be a haphazard fashion as he travels forward on his journey. All that he was attached to, all that he might have thought would keep him afloat in times of uncertainty—the life raft of his retirement plan, or of the youthful energy he thought would never leave him—will be carried out of reach by the swirling, gurgling waters. He must submit to rushing downstream, bobbing along without fearing what will become of himself or all the things he'd hoped would be his permanent possessions. The marriage, the job, the identity as a rebellious iconoclast, and even the vision of himself as being immortal and in perfect health may all have to be surrendered. He trusts that these treasured items may return to him someday;

EXERCISE: Cleansing Your Chakras with Water

You can practice this exercise in the morning while in the shower, or in nature by a waterfall, a stream, or the ocean. Hold your left hand at the base of your spine, and with your right hand three or four inches above your pubic bone area, "feel" for your first chakra. You might feel it as a cool or tingling sensation. Spin the chakra counterclockwise (imagine that your body is the face of the clock) three or four times, rotating your fingertips in a circle. Rinse your fingers in the water. This washes away the sludge and toxins that adhere to the walls of the chakra. Repeat for the second chakra, located two inches below your navel; for the third chakra at your solar plexus; for the fourth chakra at the level of your heart, in the center of your chest; for the fifth chakra at the hollow of your throat; for the sixth chakra at the center of your forehead; and finally for the seventh chakra at the top of your head. Make sure you rinse your fingers between rotations. Try to sense the dense energies, like cotton candy, of a chakra that is congested, in contrast with the tingling, light vibration of a clear chakra.

Now go back to your first chakra, spinning it clockwise three or four times. Repeat for all seven chakras, balancing them and reestablishing their proper direction of spin. This exercise allows each chakra to spin at its optimal frequency, unencumbered by the sludge and stale energies that cause disease at a subtle level. A clean chakra is able to draw in the energies of nature to nourish your luminous energy field and maintain optimal health.

---

and if not, they will be replaced by something greater. He looks forward to discovering what awaits him downstream when he finally reaches the gentle, lapping waters of the sea. Yet within this invisible stream he is also able to experience infinity, or timelessness. So while he is rushing down the rapids toward his old age, he is also aware of the many times he has been born and died before this lifetime and how his essence will survive beyond the end of his physical existence.

Fire is the other great symbolic element featured in initiation ceremonies. We have all seen *National Geographic* documentaries of African ceremonies around a bonfire. And in South America, the first European explorers saw how the Fuegian Indians gathered around immense fires, in the place that became known as Tierra del Fuego, "Land of Fire" in Spanish. People have always been captivated by the power of fire to keep the darkness of night at bay and to transform whatever it touches. As the wood is consumed by the flames, it leaves behind ashes that feed the earth. The flames seem to leap to the heavens, releasing the spirit from the timber. Symbolically, fire burns away what is false and leaves behind our essential self. Shamans realized that when you put a log into the fire, you were setting free the bands of sunlight that had wrapped themselves around the trunk of the tree as the earth turned around the sun. Mythic initiations relied on the symbol of fire to represent shedding our outer form and letting our inner light shine as we are "baptized by fire."

EXERCISE: Baptism by Fire

In this exercise you will bring the light and warmth of the fire into your chakras in order to nourish them with light. You can do this with a bonfire, a fireplace, or even a candle. I often do this exercise while I am on the road, using a pure beeswax candle in my hotel room. As you sit before the fire, recall the great journey that the branches in your fire have made—from seed to seedling, to bush to tree. Imagine how it blossomed in the springtime, turning sunlight into bark and leaves and roots, how it was later cut into firewood, and how that light is now returning to the night sky and the stars. Similarly, if you are sitting before a candle, imagine how honey bees labored to produce the wax out of their own bodies—a secretion used to build the honeycombs in which they keep their food and tend their larvae. To produce one pound of wax, a bee must consume about eight and a half pounds of honey, which in turn is produced by collecting the nectar from some 17 million flowers. Expand your imagination to connect yourself with the vast web of life, of which this candle is one small part.

Breathe regularly and deeply as you do this, and when you are ready, reach out with your hands and pass them around the fire. Shamans actually pass their hands through the fire, for they believe that once they have invited all of nature into their ceremony through their visualization, the fire will no longer burn them. But I want you to practice this exercise safely, so just cup your hands near the flame and imagine that you are scooping up handfuls of firelight. Now bring these scoops of firelight to each one of your chakras. Begin with the first chakra, at the base of your spine, and work your way up. If possible, do this exercise with your shirt open so there is nothing between your skin and the firelight. Be careful not to get too close to the fire or burn yourself.

Surrendering to the Flow

What if you didn't have to wait for a frightening diagnosis to begin living the way you'd like to live? What if you were willing to give up everything you know and are comfortable with, right now? You're going to have to, someday. Each of us, as mortal human beings, already has a terminal prognosis; we just try not to think about it. We figure we have plenty of time to get our life back on track and reclaim all that we're nostalgic for—but we're fooling ourselves.

During your initiation, you must be ready to enter the great unknown and experience the flood of emotions that comes with letting go of everything except faith. The good news is that when you let go of the need to battle the swirling waters, you actually discover your power to steer the course of your transition. If you resist change, you'll be caught in a whirlpool and dragged beneath the waves. You have to be willing to give up your notions about what you need in order to feel happy, whether it's public recognition of your accomplishments, a reward for all your hard work, or justice to correct a perceived wrong done to you by someone else. In becoming one with the river of timelessness, you start to recognize that the force that's carrying you along is creative and open to suggestions, yet like a whitewater river, it cannot be controlled. Once you understand this, events no longer just happen *to* you. You don't wonder, "How did I end up in this spot?" and try to fight the currents. You surrender to the initiatory process and engage with it with childlike curiosity and courage.

During a time of transition, although you may not feel very playful, laughing at your predicament will help you get past your resistance. The secret to lightening up is to stop taking the situation personally. Good humor about the existential predicaments we all face will remind you that the power to guide your transformation is also part of your human heritage.

I remember a friend of mine who was handed a terminal diagnosis by his doctors, and he was outraged. How could God do such a thing to him, when he had so much important work still to do? Why should he have to leave everything he worked so hard for just when he was about to reap his harvest? After exhausting all these questions, my friend finally made up his mind that he would not wait for the Grim Reaper to tear everything away from him; instead, he would voluntarily die to it all that very day—to his possessions, his self-importance, his attachments to relationships, and his personal history. He managed to let everything go and spent a most beautiful six years of his remaining time enjoying life with his family and loved ones.

Anytime we resist an initiation, experiencing our emotions only superficially, within the context of our old stories, we reinforce our previous distorted view of the world. Having missed the chance to move on and grow, we become more entrenched in our beliefs about how unfair the world is and make ourselves fodder for the seven deadly emotional forces. But if we have the courage to undergo our initiation, we will die in peace or live in peace, and nothing will ever frighten us as much again. The first step is to stop denying that there is a problem.

Now let us look at the seven emotional forces we must defeat during initiation. These emotions can bleed us dry unless we remedy them with the seven corresponding qualities of the higher self.

CHAPTER 6

Seven Demons and Seven Angels

There are things that can be known but not told.

I always thought that these "things" were the great bits of wisdom of the shamans. But they are not. There are no secrets in the spiritual traditions. The only secrets are the things we keep from ourselves, the terrible shame that dulls one into forgetfulness. The things I have never told anyone, not even myself.

Last night, they came to haunt me during my dreams. Demons live inside of me. Everyone has them, I suppose. In the years I spent studying psychology, I came to understand how my childhood had left deep marks in my soul. The revolution while I was a young boy in Cuba. An old woman in the early morning washing blood from her driveway with a garden hose. My father being gone during these terrible times. But these were not the demons, they were simply the events that invited these entities in to haunt me. It was the shit that had invited in the flies. The demons were my fear, the way I manipulated those who tried to love me. My selfishness and greed. I could never have enough, and so I had nothing. These were my festering wounds, and the demons were drawn to the dung in my heart.

They came to me in my dream, as guests at a feast that I'd prepared, and they kept feeding off scraps of food that fell off my plate.

"We are your only friends," one of them said. "We give you purpose. You battle us daily to heal yourself."

"Like Don Quixote and his windmills," *I thought.*
"Who else will you share your meal with?"
I woke up bathed in sweat.

Journal

Madre de Dios River, Peru

The Seven Deadly Sins, a famous painting by the medieval artist Hieronymus Bosch, captures the destructive power of wrath, greed, lust, sloth, envy, gluttony, and pride, depicting them as demons that latch on to humans, luring them, beguiling them, and eventually dragging them into lives of despair. Today, we understand that these demons are psychological forces, the result of viral programs operating in our primitive brain. Yet, when we're in the grip of lust or envy or any of the other deadly sins, it can feel as if we're being manipulated by forces greater than we are. Remember how consumed with jealousy you were when you discovered your lover was corresponding with a "secret" friend? Or how angry you were when you found out you had been betrayed by a colleague? We cannot help but long for that person that we met yesterday that was so gorgeous and magnetic. Given the power and sway these emotions hold over us, I will opt in this section for the more poetic description of these forces as "demons" that we must banish.

Christians once believed that demons were fallen angels, and that the greatest of them all, Lucifer, was once God's favorite. In fact, the name Lucifer literally means "light-bearer." In the Old Testament, demons are portrayed as important players in God's plan of creation. They were emissaries bringing tests from God, which one had to face and hopefully emerge victorious from. It is only in the New Testament that evil and the devil acquire new roles, this time conspiring against God himself. One of the most revealing tales about the demons in the Bible is the story of Job, in which Satan approaches God and proposes to challenge Job's faith. The demon wagers with God that he can break the faith of his most beloved servant, and God accepts the bet, with the condition that

Satan can do anything to Job's friends and family, but must not harm the man. Although Job loses everyone and everything he loves, his faith remains unshakable, and he is rewarded by God.

Biblical stories are not a chronicle of historical events. They are sometimes best studied as metaphors for the challenges that we may face in our human journey. Demons appear to us today much as they did to Job. When we fail to practice peace, we are overcome by anger; when we're not generous with ourselves and others, we may be possessed by greed. These faults that bedevil us feed upon our vitality and sanity, but we can overcome these demons with our inner angels by activating the circuitry of our higher brain.

The seven deadly sins arise out of a primordial need to ensure our survival no matter what the cost. Beliefs such as "I'd better get my share before it's too late" are rooted in our most basic self-preservation drives, although, to the person we elbow out of the way, it probably seems that they're based in severe character flaws. Wrath, greed, lust, sloth, envy, gluttony, and pride are found in the animal world, although never to the degree of excess we see among humans. Crows will steal from each other's nests, hyenas will gorge on a wildebeest until they can hardly move, and eagles are known to hunt for the largest salmon running upstream—to the point that they are unable to fly off with their prize and have to use their wings like paddles to wade ashore.

In contrast, the seven virtues are the attributes of our new brain, which is able to shed the fear of death, replace the nightmare of scarcity with a sense of abundance, perceive our immortality, and experience a sense of oneness with creation. By courting the seven angels of light, we rise above the grip of our more brutish survival instincts. We are able to collaborate with each other and not just compete. These demons haunt corporate hallways as well as human hearts. For years Mercedes-Benz and BMW have been in talks to pool their research efforts to develop more efficient and innovative engines. Their scientists understand that neither company has the resources to do this on their own, and that their survival might depend on their ability to share technologies and collaborate. But senior management was too preoccupied that the other automaker would steal their breakthrough technologies, and trounced the deal, perhaps sealing the fate of both companies.

Sometimes people are drawn to a spiritual or religious life, away from worldly temptations, but they soon realize that the demons continue to rage inside the cloister walls. Since these demons are the projection of our psychological reality, negative forces exist everywhere in the world and seem to follow us wherever we go. Make no mistake, these forces can be highly seductive and destructive. Some of the most respected priests, gurus, and spiritual teachers have slipped into gossip, arrogance, and predatory sexual behavior.

Managing Demons

We succumb to the seven demons whenever we operate from the baser instincts of the limbic brain—the taboos programmed into our hardware over the course of a million years of evolution. These taboos produce automatic responses to both real and perceived danger, as well as societal beliefs that ensure our continued existence. They are basic values that keep us from living like savages. Taboos encode the primitive rules of society into neural networks, deeply embedding these laws into everyday behavior.

With the dawn of writing, these taboos were encoded into moral law. Perhaps the best known examples are the Ten Commandments. In olden days, breaking any of these commandments brought swift and severe punishment. If you stole, your hand might have been cut off. If you practiced incest, you might have been stoned to death.

Still today, when you break one of the taboos, you feel deep shame and may be subjected to severe punishment. It is notable that prisoners convicted of sexual abuse against children are often shunned or violently attacked by the other inmates. And Jeffrey Dahmer, who violated the taboo against cannibalism, was murdered while serving his sentence.

So why would we want to override the ancient neural pathways and taboos that held the fabric of our society together for so long? Because they no longer work. They have not changed with changing society. So today the old taboos don't hold force in our society. We break commandments daily. We worship idols, use the Lord's name in vain, covet our neighbor's spouse or possessions, commit adultery, work on the Sabbath, and readily dishonor our mothers and fathers.

When the old taboos no longer hold a society together, the limbic brain—which operates best with taboos and rules—panics. It no longer knows the rules and feels that its survival is threatened. It exercises the right to vote but elects the candidate who promises to make everything familiar and okay again. It proposes a $20 billion rescue plan for General Motors to save a few jobs fabricating unsustainable products, rather than funding the United Nations hunger relief program with the $11 billion it needs to help eliminate world hunger. When old cultural taboos break down, the end of the world seems to be at hand.

The new brain, by contrast, works best with ideas. It abhors archaic rules and sets out to find the exception or break them whenever possible to break down old taboos. Such was the case when women demanded the right to vote and to practice professions once considered the province of men.

Throughout history, when the noble values of the higher brain infused a culture and a nation, they were repeatedly squashed by greedy men who lusted after power. For example, during the 15th century, the Mediterranean city of Valencia in Spain was a thriving intellectual and arts center, where Muslims, Christians, and Jews lived side by side and exchanged ideas peacefully. The universities there were the finest of the age. Then, as the Renaissance was catching on in Italy, Valencia fell into the hands of extremist Catholics who launched a counterreformation against the Protestant movements. Valencia subsequently became one of the strongholds of the Inquisition. The Moors were expelled from the city, throwing it into economic disarray, since they were the primary farmers and merchants of the area. While many people today envision the advent of a future wisdom society, one can't help wondering whether attempts to found one will encounter the same kind of resistance and reaction that the city of Valencia experienced.

Whenever we give in to lust and greed and the stories that feed them, we engage in what have traditionally been called "sins," but which we now cynically refer to as "inevitable compromises." We give in to sexual excess, overeating, hoarding, and so on, justifying ourselves with the aid of a culture that supports these behaviors in many ways. Thinking we can somehow use these demons to our advantage, we become oblivious to how we're perpetuating the dog-eat-dog mentality. Unchecked, these sins keep us in the world of hunter and hunted, fighting to survive, terrified of being devoured even as we're consumed ourselves.

An acquaintance of mine has a very demanding job as a senior vice-president in a financial institution. She does the job of three people and is unappreciated by all the colleagues who depend on her, including her boss. To top it all off, she is raising two teenage girls as a single mother. This woman jokingly refers to herself as the "walking breast" that everyone feeds off. Her schedule is wearing her down to the point of compromising her health, yet she doesn't know how to live differently. Although her constant feeding of others might appear selfless, it is really another expression of the demon of gluttony, because what she is really feeding so compulsively is her own self-image.

The seven deadly sins create psychic wounds that attract parasitic creatures seeking to feed off us. Once, while doing field research in the Amazon, I tripped on an abandoned animal den and got a nasty gash in my leg. It was a fairly deep cut, and I was a good two days downstream from the nearest clinic. I bandaged myself as best I could and began the long trek back to get assistance. Even though I applied antibiotic ointment every few hours, flies kept buzzing around and landing on my bandage, eager to feast on my dried blood. By the time I arrived at the clinic, there was green life growing on my wound. I had become a living biology experiment! In a similar way, we attract and provide nourishment to parasitic people by allowing our psychic wounds to remain unhealed. These individuals are not bad people; they are simply acting out of the base programming of their primitive brain.

It's like the fable of the scorpion and the turtle who meet at the river's edge. Unable to swim, the scorpion pleads with the turtle to ferry him across the river on her back. The turtle refuses on the grounds that the scorpion will sting her and she'll drown. "But why would I do that?" says the scorpion. "Then both of us would go under." Unable to refute this logic, the turtle agrees. Sure enough, when they are halfway across the river, the scorpion stings her. When the outraged turtle demands to know why he did this after arguing so convincingly that he wouldn't, the scorpion replies: "I couldn't help it. It's just my nature."

Wounds will drain until a new layer of skin is formed. Become aware of these demons, and you'll learn how to quickly close off these lacerations to avoid parasitic relationships. The seven deadly sins have been identified by every religion. To banish these demons we have to address the nature of the injury itself, the psychic wound that occurred when we failed one of our initiations. They are healed as we summon the positive forces or angels, whose light and power can defeat the demons that weaken us.

Our demons and angels are:

- Wrath, conquered by Peace
- Greed, conquered by Generosity
- Lust, conquered by Purity of Intent
- Sloth, conquered by Courage and Effort
- Envy, conquered by Compassion for Oneself and Others
- Gluttony, conquered by Temperance
- Pride, conquered by Humility

These demons latch on to us whenever we undergo one of our initiations superficially as a biological passage, or casually as a new job or marriage, while missing its mythic significance. When we experience our initiations archetypically, we awaken the angelic forces within us, and they defeat the emotions that haunt us. The story of Jesus' trials in the desert, told in the Gospels, is a classic example of archetypal initiation. For his passage into his ministry, following his baptism Jesus fasted for 40 days and confronted the demons that came to tempt him. In one of these trials, the tempter took Jesus to a mountaintop from where he could see all the kingdoms of the world in their magnificence. The tempter said, "All these I will give you, if you will fall down and worship me." This temptation of Christ is an allegory of the material temptations we all face, and often succumb to, unlike Jesus, who banished the demon by saying, "Away with you!"

There's no way to master these demons, enlist them in our service, or get the better of them. Being more artfully greedy than a business rival may boost our bottom line for a while, but in the end it leaves us feeling like a hollow shell. It's only when we bravely embrace our life initiations that we lift ourselves out of the hostile world where we're always serving as lunch for someone, whether it's a fierce carnivore or a competitor whose edge is sharper than our own. Once we're firmly ensconced in the realm of the creators, and triumph over the predatory instincts of the prehistoric brain, we'll be done with therapy forever and be able to start healing from the damage done by telling ourselves disempowering stories. When the old temptations fall away, these demons will have been banished forever. Our anger will give way to peace, an all-consuming or unfulfilled sexuality will be replaced by intimacy, and we'll stop feeling beaten up by life. However, as long as we resist our initiations, aware of our mortality but oblivious to our immortality, hearing our calling but not heeding it, we continue to nurse festering wounds that attract those who would feed off them.

Disengaging from Battles

To deactivate the toxic neural pathways, you must take seriously the power of the demons that cause your suffering. You need to be mindful of when you gravitate toward those who would seduce you into commiserating with them, with exhausting platitudes such as "No one appreciates us" and "You can't trust anyone these days." The support of well-meaning peers can entice you into allowing yourself to be sucked into the dark woods where the demons prowl about, sniffing for wounded soldiers like you. The partner or friend who promises you'll feel much better once you gain a little more influence in the world, a better-looking or wealthier mate, and a thinner waistline—or who encourages you to feel vindictive—is feeding your fear, anger, and greed. Don't we all know someone whose emotional support feels like an act of kindness but somehow always leaves us feeling more cynical and depressed about the futility of it all?

Your real allies are the angels of virtue, who in the folktales of old swoop down, assist you in tending your wounds, and pump you up with confidence and faith, gifting you with the ability to laugh. They guide you toward love, compassion, and understanding. Friends, mentors, teachers, and healers can help you call in the angels, or you can open the door for them yourself. Basking in the company of these angels by practicing their virtues will help you tap the neocortical capabilities that bring healing and grace.

As soon as you look at yourself with compassion, you can begin to weave together the tissue needed to close your wounds. The demons retreat as the angels rush in, and the dramatic tension disappears. Your ego may pout at its loss of a starring role in a major drama, but your soul will be delighted at the serenity you've created. Then you can act, unfettered by grandiose fantasies about saving the world. You can take meaningful action without demanding to know how and when your vision will manifest, or trying to coerce the universe into following your plan.

Don't Get Fooled Again

There's no way to tame the seven demons and use them to your advantage. You only temporarily satisfy a hungry ghost who will never be truly sated no matter what you achieve, acquire, or accomplish. And even when you've rerouted the toxic neural networks in your brain, the pathways will always remain. There will always be someone or something to push your hot buttons. However, once you start to dance with the angels, you no longer need to amble down the haunted hallways. This is what Christ taught when he said to turn the other cheek. He was instructing us in how to override the viral programs of the limbic brain and access the qualities of the higher brain.

Every initiation is an opportunity for healing those wounds that attract parasites. When the neocortex transcends the primitive brain's emotions, it establishes the neural holarchy and invites in the appropriate angel to help you to heal yourself from within. Then you can step back into Eden.

Next, we'll look in depth at the seven demons, their remedying angels, and the incomplete initiations that invite them into your life.

CHAPTER 7

Vanquishing the Demons of Youth

I have held misery in my arms. When I was very young, I met a woman and we were lovers. She was love itself; and by this I mean that she lived in her heart, and her heart was an open house where any invited could stay for free. I filled this house with my presence, although its design displeased me, and I feigned comfort—for it was, at least, a shelter.

I remember holding her close when we knew that it was over. I remember how it felt to embrace her grief, how her sobs, her breathless agony, shook me. I had denied her gift of love. I had taken as much of it as I could hold before my conscience forced me to stop taking.

Island of the Sun
Alberto Villoldo and Erik Jendresen

The shaman protects his personal power so he can avoid becoming worn out by the struggle with the sticky web, terrified at the approach of the looming spider. His personal power is the shimmering energy contained in the luminous field that surrounds his body. He draws on this energy whenever he's in a challenging situation, and will need to save the last of this fuel for the final days of his life, so that he may die free of debilitating disease.

The shamans say that when you have been depleted by struggling with your emotional demons, your reservoir is nearly emptied and the only energy that remains settles at your feet. They claim that they can see this energy as a shimmering light around the ankles, while the rest of the luminous field is like an empty flask. This luminous energy is the fuel that helps the shaman break out of the life that has been dreamed up for him by his family or culture, and to craft a life that's original, fresh, and meaningful for him. He will use the last ounces of this fuel at the moment of his death, during his final initiation, to make his way consciously from this life to the next. The shamans call this "getting out of this life alive." To preserve this power and retain his passion for life, he remains vigilant against the seven demons and vanquishes them whenever they appear.

Each of the seven life passages we undergo is associated with a contrasting pair of angels and demons, sins and virtues, that we must choose between. The first three demons we must defang are wrath, greed, and lust. Overcoming these forces allows us to experience the initiations of birth, adulthood, and first love at the sacred level. But if we allow their corresponding demons to prevail, we'll feel as if we "don't belong" here. We won't know love, and we'll become locked in a perpetual futile search for the answer to the question "Who am I?" Later, we'll have to face the next four demons so that we can have healthy relationships with lovers, friends, family, and community.

The First Demon: Anger, Conquered by Peace

Anyone can become angry—that is easy. But to be angry with the right person, to the right degree, at the right time, for the right purpose, and in the right way: this is not easy.

— Aristotle, *The Nichomachean Ethics*

We meet our first demon, wrath, when we are born into a world that is not safe and welcoming. The Fon people of Benin in West Africa, like in many traditional societies, consider a child to be the hope and future for the village. Thus, even before birth, a new baby is celebrated and welcomed into the family by the expectant parents, who sing and talk to the child in the womb. According to Fon folk beliefs, when a mother is pregnant, the child will peek out of the womb to determine whether the family and the village are safe places to be born into. If there's strife and domestic problems in the home, the child may choose not to be born fully. A part of him will hold back from emerging from the womb: he might be stillborn, or he'll always feel like he doesn't belong in the village.

This Fon lore mirrors the anger many of us experience toward our parents during adolescence. We feel enraged because obviously the stork dropped us off at the wrong house. And many of us remain angry for much of our lives. Wrath can be enormously destructive. When we're angry, stress hormones flood the brain; blood flow is redirected to our arms and legs, which starves our brain cells of oxygen. This biochemical assault makes it difficult to exercise good judgment and gives us the fury to lash out at perceived adversaries with great intensity. One of these chemicals, cortisol, helps us metabolize sugars needed for energy, so the initial response to anger is one of increased alertness. But cortisol, a steroid hormone produced in the adrenal cortex when we are angry, is toxic to the brain, and is especially deadly to memory neurons in the hippocampus that are loaded with cortisol receptors.

Anger can be so strong that it blinds us to our creative abilities and the many solutions to a problem available to us. The old prescription of counting to ten when we're raging addresses the need to slow down the primitive anger response. Deepening our breathing lowers the heart rate and allows the neocortex to use its executive function; override impulsivity; and access reason, compassion, and creativity. We can use words instead of our fists.

Anger fatigues us physically, emotionally, and spiritually. The neural loops in the prehistoric brain can turn us into "rageaholics," continually feeding the nasty beast with our angry thoughts and feelings even as it opens its jaws to devour us. We become consumed by our fury, and it takes every ounce of energy to keep up the mental tirade about how we've been wronged. The brain-damaging chemical cocktail it generates lowers our immune function, making it harder to ward off illness. Our wrath feeds upon itself as we tell our tale of victimhood over and over again, embellishing it with more details of just how awful our persecutor is and how badly we've been hurt or betrayed.

A traditional Hopi understands that every child has two sets of parents: a biological mother and father, as well as a pair of divine parents. In olden days, when a Hopi child was born, a perfect ear of corn was placed on her crib, to represent the Corn Mother, or Mother Earth. The ear of corn was also a reminder that her parents were simply the vehicle through which she came into the world. For the first 20 days, she was kept in darkness, because she was still transitioning from the invisible world—where she remained under the care of her divine parents—to the world of humans. Cornmeal was used to paint sacred designs on the walls and ceiling of the house, to represent that a spiritual home as well as a physical home had been prepared for the child.

We find the Divine Mother in nearly all the major religions— the Madonnas of Christianity, deities such as Tara in Buddhism, the many forms of Kali in Hinduism, and the Shekhinah, or feminine presence of God, in Judaism. Our attraction to the Divine Mother and the comfort and safety she brings continues throughout life for many people. When a child is born without her protection, the demon of wrath sneaks into the cradle. If you haven't been welcomed into the world by your parents, if they did not communicate a feeling of anticipation and delight at your arrival, your worth wasn't validated, and you will become distrustful and resistant to life's unexpected twists. As an adult, when you no longer have access to a mother who can kiss away your pain, you feel like an orphan who's been cheated of your birthright. You perceive that you live in a cold, hostile place, and resent those who brought you into this strange land. You seethe in simmering anger toward your parents, holding them to blame for your misery. This demon does not wait only by our cribside. It taunts us every time we go through a symbolic rebirth. When we get our first job after college or move to a new town, we may find our dreams and enthusiasm crushed by a tyrannical boss or an arrogant teacher at our child's new day-care center.

Often, we try to befriend this demon of wrath because we believe that anger gives us power. It's true that rage is a strong force; we sense it in our bodies, and the adrenaline rush it generates makes us feel like we could defeat anyone. Angry people can be very intimidating. But when we give in to anger, we continue to foster the situations that feed that rage. We discover that we're constantly surrounded by unfriendly people, from the receptionist who makes passive-aggressive comments to the accountant who lets us know in his own subtle way that we're unworthy of his full attention. Trapped by the primitive response of anger, we unconsciously invite others to feed off our irritation and resentment.

Genuine power lies in the ability to practice peace when confronted by someone else's fury. In the martial arts, students are taught to come to tranquility in order to defeat an opponent, and to use the force of the opponent's fury against him: you step back and let your opponent fall on his own sword. So when your ex goes into the same argument for the 900th time, back off—do not engage a battle that creates exhausting dramas. Ancient samurai would not confront their enemies while angry because they knew how weakened they would be by that force. There's a story of a samurai who is sent by his lord to slay another warlord. When he arrives, the man spits in his face and insults his ancestors. At that point the samurai sheathes his sword and leaves. When his master asks why he did not slay the other man, the samurai reports: "Because I had become furious."

The angel of peace gives you the strength to let go of your self-righteous story. You're able to step back and recognize how the other person's behavior is rooted in his own pain and choose not to accept the invitation to an angry tussle. Remember, it's not the other person who's picking the fight; it is the demon, the wounded part of you, that wants to start swinging.

The only way to disengage your hot buttons is by making peace with the demon you're battling. In our culture, we think of peace as a benign, harmless state that feels nice and cozy but that won't solve the very real problems in the world. The prehistoric brain is programmed for quick anger and violence. It can be disconcerting to realize just how quickly your hands start shaking when you read an upsetting e-mail. Yet the force of peace has a strong effect too. The more peaceful you become, the easier it is to see how much energy other people waste as they carry on crusades against everyone who irritates them.

The price of peace often seems too high. No one wants to cede important ground in a negotiation, and you should never compromise your integrity. But you also don't have to hold on to all the power in a situation. Peace may cost you, but it's the price of war that bankrupts the soul.

To create peace, you have to let go of your need to be right. It's only natural to want to have both peace and victory, saying to yourself, "If she would just admit that she's wrong, *then* I'd be willing to show mercy." But the more you hold your ground, the more you become entrenched in your position, and then you're really just fighting about how awful the other person is—and you won't even remember what you started arguing about. Once you've experienced the power of peace, you won't be so quick to give it up just to be able to claim that you're right. A friend of mine once said to me during a very difficult time in my life, "Do you want to be right, or do you want to be peaceful?"

If you believe you can't experience peace until you've worked through your anger, you're wrong. The only way to work through your anger is to invite this conquering angel of light in. Psychological or therapeutic techniques can be a distraction that feeds the monster instead of slaying it. Make peace a conscious choice. Take a deep breath, smile, and as you experience equanimity, tranquility, and acceptance, you become filled with vitality and power. You remove the taps from your maple tree, and the holes in the bark begin to close. You give up the addiction to drama, and you can invite others to join you in forging a new relationship. If they refuse, you can simply walk away, reserving your energy for your own creativity.

"But how will I survive in a world where people are violent?" you might ask. When Captain John Smith (of *Pocahontas* fame) arrived off the coast of Maine, he ordered one of his lieutenants, Thomas Hunt, to load one of the ships with dried fish to bring to Europe. Hunt invited a group of friendly Pawtuxet Indians to visit his ship, and promptly absconded with more than 20 of them, whom he sold as slaves as soon as he landed in Spain. What's to keep us from a similar fate? we might ask ourselves. The shaman would answer that if you practice peace in your life, you are met with peace and avoid such terrible circumstances. At least I have found this to be true in my life.

The Second Demon: Greed, Conquered by Generosity

The demon of greed afflicts us when we fail to complete our initiation into manhood or womanhood. With the arrival of puberty, we're in the position to no longer simply take from others but to give as well. We are old enough to work and smart enough to look after the sheep or cows belonging to our family. In tribal societies, the rite of manhood and womanhood marked the time when a young person took up the hunt or the planting and gathering, and started to contribute to supporting the family. Although this initiation is associated with coming of age, we face it every time we doubt our ability to provide emotional or financial support for our loved ones or ourselves.

In his Sermon on the Mount, Jesus assured his followers that they need not worry about food and clothing, as long as they made righteousness their first priority. When you doubt that you will be provided for by the universe, unlike the birds of the air or the lilies in the field, you start to believe that the world is plagued by scarcity. Then it's natural to react by trying to take what you need before someone else has a chance to get to it, and hoarding what you have. Doubting the generosity of the universe is the essence of greed. Rather than trusting that tomorrow will provide all you require, you start making a mad grab in order to fill your stores with money, possessions, information, or whatever makes you feel powerful. A friend who worked as an assistant to a corporate executive was once verbally abused by an angry client. To her surprise, the client ended up not only apologizing but also sending a bouquet of flowers, which she didn't feel was necessary. "Lucky you," said her boss when she heard the story. "She really screwed up and she knows it. It's good that she owes you a favor, because she's got a lot of clout. You'll want to call in that favor someday." In a predatory world, trespasses and penalties are carefully weighed and the score is mentally noted for future reference.

The instinct to build up stores of power may be a good one, but the resources you really need for the challenges you'll face in life don't come from currying favor with the powerful or hoarding material things. What you need is the spiritual power you acquire through the practice of generosity. In fact, the more you are kind and giving, the more equity you acquire. The shamans of the Andes have a revealing name for generosity. They call it *ayni*, which means reciprocity in the Quechua language. They understand that the more you give to others, the more you receive in return. *Ayni* implies an active process of give and take. You offer *ayni* to the ancestors, and they give you wisdom; you offer *ayni* to Mother Earth, and she returns abundant crops. You offer *ayni* to your neighbors, and they help you rebuild when your house burns down. The way they offer *ayni* is to honor everyone and everything around them. Thus, they live in a world of abundance, regardless of how few possessions they have. *Ayni*, or reciprocity, is the way the universe works. But you must offer *ayni* for its own sake, not to get goods in exchange. Otherwise it can become a business transaction with greed at its center. We, on the other hand, fear we are living in a world of scarcity no matter how many material things we accumulate.

Without the higher perspective of our new brain, we scramble and scheme and find ourselves agreeing with that line from the

1980s movie *Wall Street:* "Greed is right. Greed works." Adam Smith, the father of modern economics, argued that "self-interest" (another name for greed) is necessary as the driving force of capitalism. We tell ourselves it makes sense to be greedy because there's not enough to go around. But is that really true? The more we believe in an unfruitful and barren world, the more we find our physical world actually lacking. According to a study released in 2006 by the World Institute for Development Economics Research of the United Nations University, the richest 2 percent of adults in the world have more than half of the world's wealth, and half of the world's adult population accounts for barely 1 percent of global wealth.[11] People in wealthy nations continue to feel entitled to use a disproportionate amount of resources compared with those in poor nations, and people in developing nations strive to increase consumption to make sure they get their slice of the pie.

When we're in a greedy frame of mind, we may recognize that planting, teaching, healing, and helping others are all noble pursuits, but we won't make time for them unless we can see a big payoff or the chance to receive credit for our charitable behavior. We keep postponing our good deeds, and instead we focus on getting what we want, right now, even if we have to pry it out of someone else's hand like a Black Friday shopper desperate to get the latest bargain-priced electronic toy. Like crazed squirrels, we run around gathering every nut in sight.

Greed can only be remedied by its opposite—generosity. We find the courage to be generous when we know that if there seems to be a shortage of something in our lives—whether money, love, or time—it's our perception that's flawed. We can always grow more corn, become more loving, and make time for ourselves and others. Giving generously is easy when we recognize that giving doesn't deplete us. In fact, giving to others can actually make us feel rich. The more we give of ourselves, especially of what is valuable to us, the more the universe provides for us.

The demon of greed can be very tricky. He'll latch on to you again if you make too much of your generosity and feed your ego with thoughts like "Aren't I a fantastic person for making this huge sacrifice?" Give anonymously, without expectation of credit, and you won't feed this demon. Give of yourself, your time, and your compassion without any ulterior motive. Real generosity means calling an old friend to find out what's going on instead of just picking his brain for information you can profit from.

We don't have to live in a world of competition, accumulation, and scorekeeping. When I was on a swim team as a teenager, I hated the pressure of having to beat my competitors in the other lanes. If I won, the victory did not last for long; if I lost, I was depressed all day. It wasn't until I began competing with myself, trying to better my own times and not worrying about how well anyone else was swimming that I really started enjoying the sport and performing better than I ever had before.

Like the hunter who recognizes that we're all part of the web of life, a shaman finds balance between giving and receiving. She doesn't exhaust herself trying to be all things to all people in order to win their approval. She also doesn't go on a rampage, trying to bully, cajole, or use people in order to get ahead in a competitive world. A creator doesn't crush opponents. She sees that all such actions will keep her out of the fertile world of prosperity.

Becoming generous allows us to take care of ourselves while at the same time assisting others. We no longer narcissistically insist that the world meet our demands. We stop expecting our boss to be the nurturing parent that Mom or Dad never were, or insisting that our romantic partner make us feel happy and secure. We undergo this initiation and become fully men and women many times during our lives.

Banishing the demon of greed, we find a balance between giving and taking. We give what we can and take only what we need from our loved ones and our community, and from the earth.

The Third Demon: Lust, Conquered by Purity

The demon of lust appears when we fail to complete the initiation of first love. In the age of sexual freedom, lust as a "sin" is often perceived to be a quaint and even ridiculous notion; yet experience shows that looking at others as sexual objects, with lust in your heart, can consume you.

We talk about the value of having a "lust for life," and living richly and sensually, but that isn't lust, it's passion—an energizing force. Lust is a hopeless desire for someone—or something—you feel you can't have or don't deserve. It makes you feel deprived because you'll never meet the person who can live up to your fantasies or afford the house that can live up to your expectations. When "in lust," what a person desires most is not a union of equals but power in the relationship. Surrendering to love is terrifying to those who crave control. Men who are generous yet unable to surrender to love will focus on their lover's pleasure to the degree they are unable to receive from their partners, and this becomes a self-imposed form of punishment.

Lust is not confined to sexual desire. We can also lust after power and turn into the alpha male or the queen bee, seducing and manipulating others into giving us what we want. Like spiders, we entice them to come closer in the hope of snaring them in our web. Lust causes us to barter sex (or something else of value) for approval, admiration, or security. Inevitably, what we attract is other predators, who may pretend to be dazzled by us but are just as needy and devious as we are. I have an acquaintance who was raised in a very poor family. Although he has become very successful, whenever he meets someone he thinks is powerful or rich, he becomes subservient to this important person. His entire demeanor changes, and he loses confidence in his own merits and achievements. He is so awed by the rich people he tries to impress that even I no longer know who he is in these situations. And the most astonishing part is that he is totally unaware that his behavior changes when he starts kissing up to the powerful. Of course, these people find him dull and uninteresting, since they're surrounded by yes-men, and he's just another gushing admirer in their eyes.

Uninitiated lovers only experience sex carnally, and their minds create false beliefs about real intimacy. Awash in a sea of emotions, they become convinced that every one-night stand is the beginning of a deep relationship with their one true soulmate. They insist they're victims of Cupid's arrows, or they deny that their emotional and sexual behavior is predatory. They never experience a deep intimate connection, nor are they able to step back and free themselves from the object of their desire. When someone resists the call of love and the surrender to a true union, his interactions—whether friendships, family relationships, or business partnerships—are all centered on "What's in it for me?"

When you're initiated into love, your relationships are about discovery and openness, not exploitation. I have a friend who loses all interest in a partner after he sleeps with her. He explained to me one time that after the conquest, the woman ceases being a mystery to him, so he leaves her. When he finally met a woman he really liked, he was afraid to become physically intimate because he didn't want to repeat the pattern and end up losing her. Meanwhile, his partner was mystified and began to suspect that there was something wrong with him. Of course, my friend is mistaking purity for chastity. He doesn't know how to approach his beloved as if it were his first time.

Our culture teaches us that we have to market ourselves like products in order to attract the partner we desire. Everything from book titles to trends to product packaging must be "sexy," according to this mentality. Hoping to "bag" a partner and "win over" others, we'll boast, preen, shake a tail feather, or display our bodies with an air of nonchalance. But it's our purity of intent that attracts emotionally healthy partners.

To practice purity of intent is to have a willingness to trust, and to enter partnership with truthfulness and curiosity. Creative power throbs within us when we're sincerely engaged in our interactions and explorations—not when we're trying to seduce or micromanage them. If we practice purity, we're able to stop worrying about how we look and how we're performing, and whether others think we're lovable, desirable, or powerful. We can discover the unknown potential of relationship, whether in a sexual, romantic, social, or business situation. We're no longer a tiger on the prowl, searching for a mate in order to spread its seed and ensure the survival of its genes. Instead, we become "virginal," looking through the eyes of the soul instead of the eyes of the hunter. This purifies our interactions from the taint of lust.

If we don't successfully undergo the initiation that love offers us again and again in life, we resist taking risks, hold fast to our need to control, and focus on gaining power over others. Then we wear ourselves out trying to seduce everyone in sight in the vain hope of filling the void in our self-esteem.

If we are a man or woman who has fully surrendered to the mysteries of love, we are ready to forge healthy adult relationships. We no longer struggle with self-worth and are ready to create partnerships, bring forth children or creative projects, and contribute to the community. Not blaming our parents, expecting others to take care of us, or trying to force the world to conform to our myopic vision, we are ready to conquer the next four demons.

CHAPTER 8

Vanquishing the Demons of Maturity

In all the countries north of the equator—and remember that the great cultures of history developed north of the equator—God is a descending god. Think of the Greeks, the Romans, the Christians, the Muslims. The Divine comes from the heavens and descends to the Earth . . . But for the Incas, the only great culture to develop south of the equator, the god-force is ascending. It rises from the Mother Earth . . . rises from the Earth to the heavens like the golden corn.

And those who are buried here at Sillustani (at Lake Titicaca, the Sea on Top of the World) are the men and women who spent their lives acquiring knowledge, germinating and cross-germinating their wisdom and their corn, discovering and understanding the forces of Nature and the relationship between the Sun and the Earth and the Moon and the stars. They practiced a way of knowing that is . . . an alchemy of life. The alchemy of your European ancestors consisted of taking dead matter— base elements like sulphur and lead—and placing it in a crucible and applying fire in a vain effort to make gold. But my people used living matter, placed it in the crucible of the Earth, under the fire of the Sun, and produced corn, a living gold.

Island of the Sun
Alberto Villoldo and Erik Jendresen

After you have passed the first initiations, you are ready to confront the demons that can keep you stuck at the thresholds of marriage, parenthood, sagehood, and death. These four initiations are part of maturing and becoming a member of a community. Vanquish these demons, and marriage will not mean losing your freedom, nor will having a child mean losing your youth. You can stop trying to get the world to conform to your wishes and whims. And you can approach the great crossing to the realm beyond death fearlessly and with grace.

We go through these initiations many times in our lives, and not only at the biologically appointed moment. Anytime we have to commit to a path or a project that requires our unwavering dedication, we face the initiation of marriage. If we end a marriage, change career paths, or lose a loved one, we must undergo the death rites.

The person who conquers the demons of sloth, envy, gluttony, and pride has the wisdom to know when to act and when to accept a situation as it is. Her prince doesn't turn back into a frog with intimacy issues after the third kiss, and she doesn't see him as "the problem" but rather faces conflicts as an opportunity to have a healthy relationship at last. She refuses to cast herself as a victim in a drama called, "Can you believe a nice girl like me puts up with a guy like him?"

It's in these last four initiations that we start awakening to our mortality and the fact that we will not be around forever. Yet with each initiation, the realization of our infinite nature also starts to dawn on us, allowing us to age gracefully. Otherwise, we become embittered and jaded with advancing years. The awareness of our immortality will be a necessary realization to successfully complete the final initiation, the great crossing.

After your immortal self begins to stir from its deep slumber, you start to develop a spiritual resilience. Whenever you face hardships, you'll recall that this is just a drama playing out, and you can either go along with it or rewrite the script. Having already faced the death of all you hold dear several times, and discovered that what remains is the true gold that the alchemist has been seeking all along, you're not afraid to enter the realm of the unknown in any aspect of your life. Living fearlessly, you soon find yourself thriving in your relationship with your beloved, engaging in a new kind of dialogue with your children, and becoming a sage instead of an "old fart." You recognize that you can't prevent the crow's feet from appearing around your eyes or the waning of your physical strength, but you also don't have to allow these changes to define who you are. You accept, detach, forgive, feel compassion for yourself and others, and agree to disagree. Eventually, you'll be able to face the Angel of Death and announce to him that you belong to Life and can never be claimed by Death.

This second half of the journey starts with battling the fourth demon, sloth, which prevents you from creating healthy partnerships.

The Fourth Demon: Sloth, Conquered by Courage

Sloth rears its ugly head when we stop growing and learning, and then life comes and takes away everything we took for granted. The Greek myth of Helen of Troy, whose story has been told primarily by Homer and Euripides, is one of the most poignant tales of what happens when you rest on your laurels. (That expression comes from the ancient Greek practice of crowning heroes with a laurel wreath; so to rest on your laurels means to rely on your past victories and to make no further efforts, owing to sloth.) Helen is the daughter of the god Zeus and a human woman of extraordinary beauty. When she comes of age, she is courted by princes and kings who bring gifts of great wealth in an effort to win her hand. Eventually she is married to Menelaus, king of Sparta, who believes that the difficult task was winning Helen as his wife, and who goes back to attend to kingly things after his betrothal. Soon after his marriage Menelaus discovers that the most challenging part of any relationship begins *after* the honeymoon. Helen is kidnapped by Paris, a Trojan prince, and taken to Troy (the land of the Trojans). Helen obviously was not up for the role as the king's trophy wife and dives into a passionate affair with Paris. If we become slothful, we soon lose everything we hold dear, like Menelaus, who has to send in an army to sack Troy and burn it to the ground in an unsuccessful attempt to recover Helen. In this story, Troy represents everything in our lives that is beautiful and refined, and that we inevitably destroy if we succumb to sloth in its various forms, such as the failure to use our talents, the refusal to work hard, ignoring or neglecting our obligations, and emotional laziness.

Every relationship or partnership involves give and take, surrender and negotiation, but we often find it difficult to do the hard work and sacrifice for the good of all who are involved. We think, "Maybe if I could just explain it differently, they'd understand and see that I'm right." A friend of mine who traveled on business for most of his children's early years keeps holding on to the thought that someday, once he's had a chance to explain how he toiled and sacrificed for the family, they'll understand that he was a good father after all. In his case, although he worked hard at earning a living, being slothful meant neglecting his family, while wistfully wishing for forgiveness from his children without making any effort to earn it. We may expend a great deal of energy trying to get others to go along with our plans, but in reality, we're being emotionally slothful and lazy.

The fourth initiation is the rite of marriage. This is the initiation we face when we're invited to commit deeply to another person, or to a partnership, venture, or cause. When we don't succeed with the fourth initiation, we expect our romantic partner to meet our every need and be the first one to say "I'm sorry," and we expect others we interact with to meet us far more than halfway. We joint-venture with a friend to develop our idea into a viable business, but we fail to "show up" at critical junctures in its growth. We give in to selfish habits, tallying up who gave more or suffered more, and strategize about how to win every argument rather than trying to create a union that transcends the parties' personal agendas.

Subsequently, we become ambivalent, wondering if the partnership is really worth the hard work. We start to daydream about the perfect mate we should have married or who might be just around the corner—the ideal woman or man who puts up with all our flaws and never complains. Or we imagine that the deal we are working on is not the right one after all, that it is the next one that will help us break through. Fantasizing is much easier than working to improve an actual relationship.

Sloth is about expecting that all we've worked for and achieved will last forever because that's what we deserve. We feel entitled to put our feet up and enjoy the fruits of our labors. After all, during the courtship we listened with our full attention, made the effort to treat our partner with kindness, and kept our stomach muscles tightened. Now that the honeymoon's over, all that takes too much energy. Our niceties and manners, our gentleness and acceptance, have been replaced by demands. Our attitude is "My day was much harder than your day, so *you* make dinner," and "I know we're both feeling exhausted, but I'll wait for you to be the one to breathe life back into our partnership."

In our state of sloth, we wish we could go back to the days of romantic evenings, the champagne toasts, and the giddy feeling of discovery and passion again, but we know we can't regain what we've lost. Memories keep us frozen in place. We wonder what happened to the person we married and wish things could return to how they were. And when they don't, we end up like an acquaintance of mine who recently said to me, "I miss the man I married, not the one I'm divorcing." When the demon of sloth has us under its spell, we don't want to have to get used to something new, even if it seems to hold some promise. This same woman who was going through a divorce told me, "I can't stand the idea of being single and dating again at 40!"

Sloth creates a pessimistic attitude and a belief in the futility of your actions. This attitude will suck the energy right out of you and doom your partnerships with others, and your ability to serve any cause no matter how strongly you believe in it or how loudly you espouse it. The more you finger your high school trophies or lament the loss of your "dream" marriage or job, the more you blind yourself to the possibility of creating something better. Nostalgia sets in to distract you. You flee the responsibility of working on the partnership out of fear that that it can't be fixed, and avoid committing to a cause for fear it might be doomed.

Slothfulness keeps you on autopilot. Even if you're very busy, you're accomplishing little of substance. Your endless discussions with your partner never seem to solve any of your problems, and your days of planning and scheming with your best friend do not result in the new venture of your dreams. You attend a half dozen weekend workshops and set up meetings with mediators to get your partnership back on track where you'll frankly admit to your failings, but you can't seem to muster the impetus to transform. You wish someone would wave a magic wand and fix it all for you.

Slothfulness happens not just at a physical level, when we refuse to act, but at an emotional and mental level, too. We allow ourselves to be drained by sorrow and disappointment and become too sluggish or too enamored of our own ideas to explore anything new. We're incurious and let life happen to us or pass us by. Days turn into weeks, months, and years as our lives and relationships stagnate. When we're slothful, we assume there's nothing left to discover. We don't want to question, think too hard, or experience ambivalence or uncertainty. Despite our insistence that we'd like to move forward, we remain stuck because we've allowed our creativity and passion to leach out of us.

Making empty promises and indulging in avoidant behaviors that distract you from what you really should be doing is slothful, even if doing so keeps you very occupied. But life doesn't have to be this way. All your efforts can be part of a creative process in which you playfully engage with the world and tickle the underbelly of the universe and make it smile. Courage, the remedy for sloth, means following through on your finest ideas and having the courage to answer the call of your soul. It means discarding the selfish need to get someone else to fashion a partnership, project, or situation that will make you feel fulfilled and energized, and investing the enthusiasm and creativity into it yourself. Courage means you willingly engage in negotiations and conversations that foster intimacy. You're committed to sticking with a partnership instead of dropping out the moment the thrill is gone, because you know you can bring back the vitality. Doing what needs to be done without pouting, or spinning a story of how you deserve a better life or a better partner, stops you from being sucked dry by sloth.

Courage is associated with marriage because a strong partnership requires perseverance and dedication even in the darkest of moments. The word *courage* comes from the Latin root *cor*, meaning action from the heart. Many traditions recognize the mystical phenomenon of marriage with the Divine, an inner relationship that requires great courage, as you are called to leave everything worldly behind. Catholic nuns wear a ring that represents their mystical union with Christ. There are many times that a novice falls into a dark night of the soul during which she questions her faith and calling. Even experienced practitioners who have followed a path for many years will have these moments of doubt and reflection. It's during such moments of bewilderment that courage is most needed to help us make our way through the forest to the clearing on the other side, and to a renewed faith and dedication to our path.

Even if you are not in a religious order, you can forge a mystical marriage in the alchemical sense. The sacred marriage in alchemy symbolizes a reconciling of opposites within the personality, by means of making internal conflicts conscious and integrating them into a harmonized sense of self. These opposites are most often portrayed as the inner masculine and feminine, what Carl Jung would later call the *anima* and the *animus*. When these apparent opposites are integrated, one's false ego falls away and one unites with the Divine. This requires great daring and courageous action.

The mystical union in which one's false ego falls away and one unites with the Divine requires daring and courageous action. In one of his poems, the Sufi poet Rumi writes:

There was a feast. The king
Was heartily in his cups.

He saw a learned scholar walking by,
"Bring him in and give him
some of this fine wine."

Servants rushed out and brought the man
to the king's table, but he was not
receptive. "I had rather drink poison!
I have never tasted wine and never will!
Take it away from me!"

He kept on with these loud refusals,
disturbing the atmosphere of the feast.

This is how it sometimes is
At God's table.

Someone who has *heard* about ecstatic love,
But never tasted it, disrupts the banquet.[12]

When you're courageous, you have a spiritual practice, not just
a spiritual library. You understand that all the information in the
world does you no good if you don't turn every prayer into action.
Saying, "You know me, I'm bad at expressing my emotions," just
doesn't fly when your children and spouse long to have you say, "I
love you." When you banish the demon of slothfulness, you stop
making excuses, cease exploring the origin of your discomfort
with intimacy, and bravely say what you know in your heart needs
to be said.

Courage results in tranquility without inertia, and action
without wasteful effort. If you've fully submitted to the initiation
of marriage and partnership, you're willing to work cooperatively
with others and with the universe. Instead of lazily moving

forward through life, you're able to answer your calling, and you become willing to break the mold of emotional cowardice and try something genuinely new. You don't have to go on a cruise to revitalize your relationship; you can choose to rediscover your partner that very afternoon.

To arouse the healing, vitalizing force of courage, you need to participate mindfully in mundane events, focusing on what you can do in this moment rather than sitting back and scripting yet another story that begins, "If only . . ." Then you'll be able to accept your invitation to the banquet that Rumi speaks about. If you're married, you'll choose to make a change instead of remaining in the status quo and allowing your verve to seep out of you. You'll choose to explore who you are, your relationship to others, and to life itself.

If we don't cross this threshold of partnership, we're plagued by loneliness, depression, and possessiveness. But if we can complete this rite successfully, we'll be able to love fully and feel peaceful yet passionate.

The shaman recognizes that she's on this earth to explore and experience love, and that she has to adapt to circumstances, because she's not the only one on the dance floor. She works cooperatively, dreaming with others and fashioning something new.

The Fifth Demon: Envy, Conquered by Compassion for Oneself and Others

Envy is feeling jealous of others and coveting what they have. The story of the parents of Aphrodite, the Greek goddess of love and beauty, illustrates the dangerous consequences of envy. Aphrodite was born of the sea foam after Cronus cut off the testicles of his father, Ouranos, and threw them into the ocean. Ouranus was Father Sky, both son and husband of Gaia, Mother Earth. He was so concerned that his children the Titans would usurp his place in the heavens that he imprisoned them deep inside the earth. This greatly pained Gaia, who fashioned a great sickle and asked her son Cronus, who longed for his father's power and stature, to castrate him. Cronus became associated with the harvest, cutting down the stalks of grain so that new life might arise, and was celebrated as a god of abundance. Although Cronus' envy led to the birth of the goddess of beauty, he was later overthrown by his own envious sons.

Envy is rooted in what psychologists call projection. We project the positive aspects of our shadow, or unconscious personality, onto somebody else, and think, "If only I could have his success," or "If only I could be slim like she is." This envy allows others to feed off our insecurity and desire to be important, admired, or powerful. Shamans, who often engage in magical battles on behalf of a client, know that the envy of others can be a powerful force that can make one ill. During these mythical encounters they defend their clients from a form of "psychic attack" that they believe originates from envy.

We tend to glamorize envy because we think it will inspire us to work harder and achieve more. Magazines encourage envy by suggesting that we can buy our way into looking like a celebrity, while commercials featuring movie stars and sports legends sell us overhyped products that promise to make us virile or gorgeous, and transform us into an object of envy ourselves. All we have to do is purchase the right designer shoes or sports car.

We're envious of someone else because we think he's found the magic key to fulfillment. Then we look for that person's formula for living and try to adopt it as our own, regardless of whether he's truly happy and at peace with himself—and without considering whether his formula will work for us. We dearly want to believe in the promise of becoming a superstar, but then we read stories about the scandalous hypocrisy of the famous and admired: The upstanding politician who is secretly visiting prostitutes and taking bribes. The acclaimed athlete who abuses his body with steroids. We're stunned and disillusioned to hear the truth, and wonder what went wrong with those we admired so, and even hoped to emulate.

Whenever we're in the grip of the demon of envy, we follow the footsteps of the lost and confused and wander about leading diminished lives. Thinking the payoff must be just down the road, we tag along after the object of our envy who seems to have it all, thereby blinding ourselves to our own talents and passions. Even if we're successful at plugging into the formula for happiness that was dreamed up by someone else, we end up hating the job, being disappointed in the lifestyle, or feeling trapped.

Envy is awakened early on when our own parents fail at the initiation into parenthood. Then we envy the kid next door who has the latest computer game we don't own or the family up the street whose father did not abandon them as ours did. As adults, we fail to see that our children have a destiny separate from ours. The parent who remains uninitiated spends her days driving her children from one "enrichment" activity to the next. Despite her claims that she's utterly devoted to her children's happiness and success, deep down she envies her offspring's wide-open vistas because she feels trapped herself. She tries to steer her child in a direction she's convinced will lead to success, and she ignores her own dreams and desires. The grades, test scores, and friends are never good enough for the parent driven by envy. Uninitiated parents make it very difficult for their children to undergo the initiation of birth or puberty and find their own path.

Parenthood is not only about having children, but about giving birth to something greater than you are. Have you noticed how naturally children play at being parents? Psychologists readily explain this as a desire to imitate adults or a desire to have a fantasy family without the problems at home. But it is also a deep longing ingrained in our psyche to create something larger. When we're unable to find something that we're willing to give our lives to, we're beset with envy of those who seem to have the path, relationship, or career that eludes us. At its core, envy is an active psychic attack on another: a preemptive strike. If you give in to this demon, you'll find yourself gossiping and judging others, tearing them down so that you can feel superior. We all love to be on the inside track of the latest bit of gossip, but be mindful: even listening to gossip is participating in an act of violence against the person you are hearing about.

To remedy envy requires compassion for yourself. Only when you accept yourself as you are now can you move forward into discovering what's hidden inside you, the positive shadow elements that need to be brought into the light so that they can stop serving as food for the demon of envy. You'll find that your sense of lack stems from misplaced aspects of yourself that you've been oblivious to—your own beauty, intelligence, and talents. By shining a light on these hidden assets, you can bring in the angel of compassion and stop beating yourself up for not being as good as others who seem to have more talent, money, good looks, or "glow." The light of compassion will reveal the dysfunction in the family you used to envy and the sadness in the person you thought of as the very symbol of success. Your eyes will open with kindness and consideration for their vulnerabilities and wounds and with appreciation for your own potential to be of service to others.

Compassion also means awareness of the suffering of others and the desire to relieve it. With the prehistoric brain it is not unusual to have the realization when we see someone less fortunate and say: "There, but for the grace of God, go I." But this is not compassion. This is simply a realization that through good fortune or circumstance you seem to have a slightly more comfortable or privileged life. Compassion requires social action. It is a call to do something about the suffering we perceive in the world. For the shaman, this means correcting wrongs that you witness, speaking up when necessary, regardless of how uncomfortable it may feel, or how much disapproval you might meet. Compassion for the shaman is not simply feeling sorry for someone, it is doing something about it.

Compassion allows you to reconcile your inner image of yourself with the face you present to the world. You no longer have to expend energy keeping up a charade. You can become a good parent to your ideas and projects and know that you'll nourish these "children" of yours rather than neglecting them or expecting them to fill a void inside of you. As you practice compassion you can become an agent of joy and peace.

The Sixth Demon: Gluttony, Conquered by Temperance

America is obsessed with food and diets. On any Sunday the *New York Times* bestseller list will have at least one, if not more, books on weight loss. But overeating is only one form of gluttony, which today has been turned from a sin into an illness, replete with concerns about cholesterol levels and self-destructive behavior. A glutton has no self-control and gives in to the desire to continually consume. King Midas was the archetypal glutton, a character who longed for wealth so much that when he was given a wish by one of the gods, Dionysus, he chose the golden touch. At first, Midas was thrilled that he could turn anything into gold. Then he realized the curse of his wish: he couldn't eat or drink anything, because it would automatically transform into the precious metal. He couldn't touch his lover, because she'd be transformed into a gold statue. All the pleasure in life vanished because of his bottomless need to have more. King Midas's gold represents the gluttonous desire to possess personal wealth, in contrast with the alchemist's quest for spiritual transformation, in which gold symbolizes enlightenment.

In our culture, where the gourmet is defined as a glutton with brains, and portion sizes at restaurants are ridiculously huge, gluttony has been reinvented as haute cuisine. Dinner plates are loaded with cheap carbohydrates in order to assure us we're getting our money's worth. When it became clear in the 1920s that Americans basically had all the consumer goods they actually needed, manufacturers had to become clever about marketing their products. They turned to advertising to entice people to buy what they didn't need and to open a line of credit with the store so that they could spend what they didn't have on goods they couldn't afford. It's hard to resist the appeal of gluttony when we're continually receiving seductive messages about how our lives will be so much better if we just take out our credit card. True happiness may indeed be priceless, but we can't buy it with a credit card.

The demon of gluttony tests us at the doorway to sagehood, knowing that we may stall there, unwilling to accept our loss of flexibility and strength, and respond to the wisdom that calls to us from the other side of the passage. Hesitating, we try to assuage painful feelings by consuming more than is necessary and reaching in vain for what we can never again have: the youthful energy, physical vitality, attractiveness, quickness, and in some cases, the health we've lost. In our anguish, we overlook the wisdom we've gained as we've grown older: the power to step back from the daily drama and disengage from it, to slow down yet remain fit, to be contemplative, and to expand our creativity in new directions.

If we pass this initiation, we'll embrace the gifts of sagehood instead of pining for the youth that's passed or worrying about the finite number of days we have left. We'll stop scurrying to amass wealth or close on a big business deal that will make up for the one we missed in our younger days. We're able to recognize that we'll continue on our journey after the death of the physical body and can embrace the time we do have instead of squandering it by trying to regain what is long gone in a vain attempt to stave off death.

The angel of temperance banishes the demon of gluttony and allows us to complete the initiation into sagehood. Temperance isn't a rigid unwillingness to experience pleasure, symbolized by the dour Prohibitionist with her battle-ax, out to smash every barrel of fun. Temperance is practicing moderation, taking only what you need, and exercising self-restraint in the face of temptation to overindulge. When you practice temperance, you don't squander your energy—or overload your credit card. You find creative and more sustainable ways to operate. You recognize when the party has stopped being fun and turned ugly.

Gluttony results when you're enslaved by the primitive brain's perception of scarcity. Remember that this brain matured when we were squirreling away roots in the cave for the long, hard winter. Temperance frees you so that you start thinking about what you'll leave to future generations instead of only what you can accumulate for yourself today. Temperance also allows you to quietly witness what's going on from the throne of the sage who has seen this film before and knows how it's going to play out, yet remains refreshingly engaged in life. Many wise youths learn temperance at an early age, realizing that their parents' ideas of success are not for them, or that their own goals in relationships and friendships are different.

To invite in the angel of temperance requires trusting in the abundance of the universe. Like the nomad who travels north to find the herds of reindeer, you judiciously limit your consumption, knowing that more will become available later. You know that a feast awaits you down the road, as does another famine, another feast, and so on.

The shaman accepts that his time is finite, but he doesn't feel anxiety about it. He is able to temper the sense of urgency that fosters gluttony. If we are like him, we exorcise that old belief that if we don't eat or act now, it'll be too late—what we long for will be sold out, never to be available again. The shaman has given up his addiction to calculating how much he owns, and doesn't need another big, important project to prove how important and influential he is. Being a creator is an awesome enough honor for him. If he doesn't receive credit for his accomplishments, he doesn't become upset. The grace and dignity that come with the initiation into sagehood more than compensate for any loss of youth. He recognizes his duty to the generations that will follow.

Temperance also means hardening our own steel. A sword is tempered by dipping the red-hot metal in ice water and hammering out the impurities. To temper ourselves means acquiring inner strength and fortitude, so that we don't stop climbing up the mountain because of a blister or give up on a relationship because our feelings were hurt. In the predatory world, people have become hard on the outside but soft on the inside. They give up when the going gets tough and look for the easy way out. To temper ourselves means to become tough on the inside but soft on the outside—and on others around us.

The Seventh Demon: Pride, Conquered by Humility

According to the story of Lucifer, told in the Book of Isaiah, the downfall of the angel of light was caused by pride. "Lucifer" became the name for the devil, but it's actually a Latin translation of a Hebrew term for the morning star. The traditional Christian story is that Lucifer challenged divine authority by daring to inhabit the highest heavens, putting himself above God, and was banished from the sky and sent down to hell. The Christian myth is a metaphor for what happens every dawn in the heavens when Venus—the morning star—sinks below the horizon when the sun comes up and outshines it.

The serpent in the Garden of Eden is said to have been a guise for Lucifer, who seduced humans into the sin of defying God by eating the fruit that awakened them to self-awareness. Of course, self-awareness is essential if you're to serve in your role as creator, because it means you're cognizant of your power to create as well as your power to destroy. It's when self-awareness morphs into pride and self-importance that it's a problem. Then you're banished to your own living hell.

Just as with all the pairings of angels and demons, humility conquers pride. The two extremes of self-absorption—too much focus on your individuality and lack of self-awareness—disappear. While the demon of pride would have you remain looking out for number one, the angel of humility lets you recognize your responsibility to serve others and dream a better dream for the world.

The shaman knows that he can accomplish anything if he's willing to let go of the need to take credit for the deed, or the desire to micromanage how his creation unfolds. He is delighted to see how what he brings to the table joins with what is brought by others, as a new recipe is invented. He doesn't need to attract sycophants who feed his ego and his illusion that he's powerful, important, and indispensable. He recognizes when someone simply wants to be near him to suck from his power, and he avoids these people.

The realization of how unimportant and inconsequential we are comes with the death of the story in which we've cast ourselves as the hero and everyone else as bit players. We are no longer blinded by our own need for greatness, nor do we overlook others' quiet acts of courage. We no longer underestimate our adversaries, nor figure they're nearly as clever as we are. We no longer become easy targets for those who can outmaneuver us.

The demon of pride will blind you to persons who are envious and greedy and hope to feed off of you. It will also blind you to those who are generous and open-hearted, the very people who could help you create what you most desire. Even if you enjoy playing the hero's role, the wheel of fortune will turn and your role in the stories you've scripted will quickly change: you'll shift from heroic rescuer to demanding dictator. All your efforts to control the story and continue being the attractive and admired leading man or lady will prevent you from celebrating life as it is.

One of the most flagrant examples of runaway pride is the notion that we are not separate from God and therefore we *are* God, and that we can simply kick back and watch the universe unfold. As we float in the gentle pool of self-absorbed bliss, focusing on how delicious it feels, we miss the opportunity to join forces with the river pushing its life-bringing waters downstream. Our dreams become daydreams that we expect to magically transform into reality. We channel-surf through life, changing friends and partners when we're no longer entertained. This is the demon of pride at work. The shaman, in contrast, recognizes that we're entrusted with the task of completing the work of creation and that we have a job to do. She embraces the idea of being "laid back," understanding that what we do matters, but that we should be at ease as we act. If we believe that being a part of God excuses us from being stewards of the earth and taking care of one another, we fall into the black hole of pride. To banish the demon of pride, we have to let go of these stories and embrace the practice of humility.

Being humble literally means being down to earth. The word comes from the Latin *humilis*, which is the root of the word *humus* and means "of the earth." Humility means being honest about what you are, so that you neither inflate nor underestimate your value. You recognize your intrinsic beauty and self-worth and are comfortable with your gifts. You don't need to hide them in the shadow. When you're aware of your inner worth, you don't have to seek your identity outside yourself or behave with false modesty. We all have important tasks to accomplish in this world, and humility allows us to do so without getting in our own way.

Emptying the mind is the ultimate act of humility, because then you can be free even of your own preconceptions. Then you can experience everything newly, as if for the first time. You let go of the cynical "been there, done that" attitude and become an explorer. The arrogant part of your nature dies along with your limiting stories. Humility allows you to be an amateur, in awe of what you might create, and to experience every situation with an attitude of "never been there, never done that." The word *amateur* means a "lover" in French. You become a lover of life, seeing and feeling things freshly, with what Zen meditators call beginner's mind.

Having died to your pride and self-importance, you approach situations like a sculptor molding clay, feeling its dampness and resistance, smelling its rich, earthy odor, and fashioning something original, organic, and beautiful.

CHAPTER 9

The Initiations of Youth

The Krobo people of Ghana in West Africa mark the coming of age of young women with a rite of passage known as the *dipo*. The *dipo* has been practiced for centuries to signal the end of one stage in life and the start of another. During the ceremony, each initiate's head is shaved and a string of red carnelian beads is strung around her waist by an older woman mentoring her through the initiation. Tied to these beads is a flowing red cloth that hangs between her legs, symbolizing the blood of her menstruation that will bring fertility and life to the village. During the three-week-long rite, the girls are largely in seclusion and under the tutelage of the grandmothers, where they learn the ways of the women, including the art of seduction, how to maintain a household, and how to dance. At the end of their preparations, they come before the Tekpete, the sacred stone that protects the Krobo people, and whose power is nurtured and increased by the young initiates as they take turns standing on it.

Each girl is accompanied by her "new mother," who will continue to serve as her mentor and guide. In this way, she releases her biological mother from these burdensome responsibilities that cause so many problems and mother issues for us in the West, and becomes an adult member of the village. The controversial practice of genital mutilation is also supported and perpetuated by elder female mentors, yet the Krobo do not practice it, and Ghana is the only country in Africa that has outlawed female genital mutilation.

The first three initiations in our lives happen during youth— beginning with our birth, continuing with our rites of manhood or womanhood, and ending with the discovery of first love.

The Rite of Birth: Peace Conquering Wrath

Birth designates the biological separation from our mother and the first taste of our identity as individuals. This initiation frees us from the sins of our fathers and the lost dreams, disappointments, and psychological issues that our parents were burdened with. When we don't cut the cord with our parents, we are unable to shed their burden of negativity or embrace their positive legacy. What the medieval Church called "original sin" might be reinterpreted in terms of what modern biologists call "epigenetic factors," the biases, prejudices, and fears passed from one generation to the next. When we fail to undergo this initiation, we acquire anger as our weapon—anger against our parents, against God, and against the uncertainty and powerlessness brought on by our genetic conditions and our childhoods. A rite of birth that welcomes us into the world gives us a sense of belonging in our families and in the world, without being possessed by either.

The birth rite does not happen automatically when we pass through the birth canal. It is orchestrated by parents who refuse to look at their children as mere extensions of themselves. If the child does not rebel against this version of reality, he'll be stuck trying to please his parents or perpetually rebelling against them. I know of a couple approaching their 80s who are dealing with Medicare, knee replacements, and downsizing to a condo—as well as playing out the same old dynamic with their middle-aged son who wants them to wholeheartedly approve of all his decisions and bail him out financially whenever the bills for those decisions come due. Until he undergoes the initiation of birth and separates emotionally from his parents, he'll determine his every move according to what he thinks they'll say, good or bad, despite claiming that he wants to be his own man. Meanwhile, his anger at the unfairness of it all consumes him. One day, when his parents finally stop lecturing and pleading with him to listen to their guidance, perhaps then he'll be able to experience the rite of birth that will free him from perpetual anger. The only difference is that this time he will have to make his own way through the symbolic dark tunnel of the birth canal as a result of a trauma such as the loss of a relationship or an accident.

The initiation of birth announces our entry into the world with a destiny all our own. We can go through this initiation anytime there is a rebirth in our lives—after a graduation from school, after the start of a new job, or after the end of a serious relationship. In fact, even our birthday celebrations are an opportunity to celebrate this initiation on an annual basis, setting new goals and direction for our lives. When we go through the initiation of birth successfully, we recognize that we have a calling to be of service to the world in our unique way—to have our particular light that we set atop a hill so that it can shine in all directions. But if you fail to make this transition, your primitive brain will insist that you assert yourself through the power of your anger. You establish a reputation as someone who should not be crossed. Perceiving others as authority figures who aren't doing right by you, you impose on your relationships a template of wrongdoer and wronged one.

After this initiation you stop living according to what you think your family wanted you to be or engaging in knee-jerk rebellions. You'll let go of anger that causes you to feel you don't really belong here.

During the birth rite, all those attending welcome you and affirm your individuality. One starry night soon after my daughter was born, I brought her to a campfire, held her squirming little body toward the earth, and prayed, "Mother, this is your child. I'm just her caretaker." Then I held her up to the heavens, saying,

"Father, let her find her own destiny, and let me help her to grow the seeds that are in her soul." I dedicated her to her divine parents, acknowledging that I am only one provider of wisdom and protection for her and that she has her own road to travel. I felt humbled by the responsibility of becoming a parent. But ushering my child into her own destiny by allowing her to look to Mother Earth and Father Sky for guidance made it easier for me to complete my own passage into parenthood. That's when I understood the adage that while you belong to your children, they do not belong to you, but to life.

A birth rite is often a naming ceremony in which the child receives a name that summarizes the dreams and expectations the community has for her. But today, we can consciously choose to rename ourselves, whenever we're entering into a new stage of life—just as an initiate into a religious order becomes Sister Catherine or Brother Joseph. A divorced woman may make up a new surname for herself, rejecting the one she had as a child and the one she had in marriage because neither seems to fit anymore. She can also take on the title of "divorce success story," which she can announce to everyone. The daughter who leaves behind her parents' expectations can replace the tag "dutiful daughter" with "woman exploring her options." Renaming oneself, literally or metaphorically, can be an important part of the "great departure" stage of any initiation.

When you claim your own separate identity, you claim your right to your dreams and stop holding others responsible for your choices. Then you discover your genuine power, the power of inner peace. When I was studying with the shamans in the Andes, I went through a series of names. The first one they gave me was a bit derogatory, "the outsider." Then, when I had my brand new Ph.D., my mentor called me *el doctorcito*, the affectionate, diminutive form of *doctor* in Spanish. Later, after I gained the respect of the shamans I was learning from, they asked me what I wanted to be called. I said my name, and they replied to me: "That is the name that was given to you by others. What name would you choose for yourself?"

I was totally at a loss. I thought of grand names like Soaring Eagle or Night Jaguar, but they laughed when I suggested them. "You are more like a squirrel," they said, because I was always taking notes and squirreling away thoughts and ideas in my notebook. So one day I said I wanted to be called Chaka Runa, which means "bridge man." To this day the shamans in the Andes refer to me by that name, because I have served as a bridge, helping to bring shamanic teachings to the West. Had I taken on a more poetic name, I might have missed out on the opportunity to align myself with a new sense of mission and purpose, with what I came to this life to do.

To complete the passage of birth in a mythic manner, you must integrate your identity as the child of your parents with your new identity as your own being. You have to discard your mother issues and father issues, recognizing that they're rebellions of the nursery and stale ways of engaging the world. Once initiated, you'll no longer feel that your behavior is a reflection on them, or that theirs is a reflection on you. Then, regardless of your age, you can be a newborn, filled with possibilities, eagerly and blissfully moving forward into your own destiny.

The Rite of Manhood or Womanhood: Generosity Conquering Greed

One of the great stories of initiation into manhood is the Greek myth of Hercules, who has to complete 12 tasks to become his own man. In his youth, Hercules killed his wife and three children in a fit of madness induced by the goddess Hera. Realizing the horror of what he has done, he consults the famous Oracle at Delphi, a prophetess who channeled the god Apollo. She tells him that to restore his honor and atone for the crime, he must serve King Eurystheus, the man Hercules despises the most because he is allied with Hera. It is the King who assigns Hercules 12 labors to complete. His first labor is to slay a monstrous beast known as the Nemean lion. Hercules prepares arrows on his way to Nemea, unaware that no weapon can pierce the lion's impenetrable skin. He thus fails to slay the beast on their first encounter. Hercules then chases the lion into its cave, where he stuns it with his club and then strangles it, using the lion's own claws to cut off its pelt. When he returns to Eurystheus, the king is awed, and Hercules is granted the indestructible skin as his prize. In all of his later tasks, Hercules wears this magical pelt and succeeds in doing the impossible, including slaying several other horrendous creatures.

The very beginning of the myth clearly shows us that Hercules is not ready for marriage and fatherhood (to put it mildly). Instead of simply leaving home, the most common way to avoid family responsibilities, Hercules kills his wife and children. He must cease being a big, bumbling brute of a boy and become a man. The lion in the story represents the fierce, primitive, aggressive nature that every man must slay lest it turn against those he loves the most. But Hercules' arrows are useless against the lion's impenetrable skin. He must meet the lion in the dark recesses of its own cave—a symbolic journey into the depths of his own soul—and there grapple bare-handed with the beast, ultimately skinning it with its own claws. Then these primitive and fearsome forces, represented by the lion's skin, serve as Hercules gifts and protection.

For a girl, the initiation into womanhood is marked biologically by her first menses, when she joins the company of women who share the mysterious power of being able to bleed without dying and to give birth to new life. In traditional agricultural societies, the young woman took her first blood to the fields, symbolizing that she was making the earth fertile and could now bring forth life from her womb in the same way the earth brings forth life from its deep, dark interior.

Yet to successfully complete this passage, the young woman must become autonomous emotionally and intellectually, which does not come with the biological passage marked by her first menses. In many non-Western societies it is impossible for a woman to become physically autonomous, and they are rigidly controlled by men. We occasionally read in the news about how a woman is stoned to death for daring to become intellectually or physically autonomous, even if this means having a profession other than housewife and mother.

This rite of passage means that she no longer belongs to her parents and is in charge of her own fertility and sexuality. In the U.S. and many other Western countries, a woman is legally subject to her parents until age 18, which is years past her menses. A teenage girl who successfully undergoes this passage no longer feels that her self-worth lies in how many men she can attract. She'll be ready to enter a relationship and give of herself without losing her freedom, because she has no secret need to retain a dependent status. She knows she can take care of herself. This is what Psyche discovers when she sets out on her nearly impossible tasks. She does not succumb to despair, although she sinks in distress many times, even when faced with the daunting task of retrieving the Golden Fleece from the fierce sheep grazing in a field. Undaunted, Psyche summons the river god, who tells her to wait until the sheep sleep at noon and collect the wool that has rubbed off on the reeds by the river's edge. The gathering of the wool was a woman's task. But during Psyche's initiation, she must collect the wool from the most dangerous of places, bring it back, and eventually spin it into cloth. The story is telling us that even in our everyday tasks we can find the opportunity for initiation. Psyche, like every woman who successfully completes the rite of initiation into womanhood, becomes self-reliant, empowered, and able to meet any situation that she faces, no matter how seemingly impossible it looks.

When my family started over again in Miami after fleeing Cuba, often the only food we had in the house was what the U.S. government had provided to us: powdered eggs, frozen vegetables, and sacks of rice and dried beans. One day, when I was a 13, a friend showed me how to fashion a simple fishing pole out of a stick and bait a hook. I walked to the pier, and after a few hours, caught a fish. It seemed huge to me, and I can recall the pride I felt as I carried it home in a sack and presented it to my mother. I beamed at the attention everyone poured over me, and after my mother had cleaned and cooked my catch, I insisted that my parents, sister, and grandmother eat first. I felt tremendous satisfaction at having brought food to my family table, and I didn't care whether I got to taste it. It was enough to see the smiles on their faces as they ate that wonderful meal I'd brought home. Many years later, I discovered that the fish I'd caught was inedible, a tropical parrot fish, and that my mother had secretly managed to get a fish from one of the neighbors to cook in its stead. They had facilitated a great rite of passage for me!

This was my first hunt, a passage out of the stage of childhood, where we're taken care of, and into adulthood, where we become members of the larger community, contributing to its survival. I'd left the company of children who depend on others and become someone who could be depended on. I'd proudly taken the first steps to transform into a man who can provide for himself and others and who has his own destiny.

American culture has rituals associated with becoming a young adult, including the sweet 16 party and the *quinceñera* (sweet 15 for Latinas), the society cotillion, the bar and bat mitzvah—and, less formally, taking a driver's test, getting drunk for the first time, or moving out of the parental home. Yet many of us never undergo the initiation required to leave childhood behind and become a contributing member of the tribe. We leave home way too late and get married way too early, oftentimes as a way to finally break the grip of the parental home and face our initiation. When we succeed in this initiation, we become aware of our stores of power and let go of the false sense of entitlement of being supported by others.

The young woman who undergoes this initiation embraces her independence and does not expect someone else to be responsible for paying the price of her life choices. The young man who completes this initiation no longer focuses only on "What's in it for me?"

The uninitiated adolescent will set out to confront the business world and vanquish his competitors, not caring about the consequences of his actions, and he'll subdue the earth with the huge carbon footprint created by his lifestyle. A young woman may do the same or follow the more traditional trajectory of the girl who doesn't cross over into womanhood but instead uses her feminine wiles to seduce others for her own advancement. The person who doesn't step into adulthood remains an unhappy, stunted creature who never overcomes the feeling of inadequacy and the fear of scarcity.

In contrast, the adolescent who has fully stepped into his manhood looks at the fish or rabbit he's caught and is humbled by having taken life in the service of life and appreciates the bounty of the earth. He recognizes that one does not kill for mere sport or glory and that if he respects the balance of nature, there will always be plenty. If a business deal of his harms the earth or a group of people, he'll find a way to compensate for what he has taken away. The young girl who has embraced womanhood has respect not only for the power of her sexuality and attractiveness and what it can bring her, but also for her power to create a life she has nurtured inside herself. She will never underestimate the value of her gifts. (Of course, these experiences of giving from a sense of plenty can be had by both genders—a woman may engage in a "first hunt," and a man may dedicate his fertility to the world.)

Finally, if you have undergone this initiation, you know you have something of value to offer to others. This passage allows a sense of purpose to emerge. You discover the personal power you had been overlooking in your quest to force the universe to conform to your needs. After this initiation, you feel content about who you are and what you can give of yourself to the world.

The Rite of First Love: Purity Conquering Lust

The pioneering anthropologist Margaret Mead caused a sensation in 1928 when she published *Coming of Age in Samoa*. The book documented how young Samoan women postponed marriage for many years while enjoying casual sex with various partners and yet eventually settled down, had children, and lived normal lives. This revelation was upsetting to many Westerners, who didn't realize that uncensored premarital sex was common in most cultures that hadn't had contact with Christian missionaries. Mead documented a practice in a society where the rite of passage of first sexual experience is not considered taboo and where young men and women can grow up with healthy attitudes toward their sexuality. Mead's work has been the subject of much controversy, including contradictions by native Samoans and a contentious book by Derek Freeman.

Ideally, the first sexual experience would bring the joy of mutual intimacy and pleasure as you share yourself with another. Yet so few people have a wonderful "first time" story that we assume that everyone must suffer a disastrous initiation into love. In reality, our initial sexual encounters are painful because so many of us have not completed our earlier initiations and aren't ready to undergo this passage. Although we are biologically ready for sex as teenagers, and many adolescents today are sexually active, the initiation of first love requires a certain emotional maturity facilitated by a tolerant society and a successful initiation into manhood or womanhood.

After this initiation, you have the power to call forth both the masculine and feminine aspects within yourself as you and your partner alternate in giving and receiving, acting and being acted upon. The masculine energy of the conquest and the feminine energy of seduction are played out sexually, and two partners complement each other's feelings and physical longings. These two energies interact to produce passion, creativity, and a delicious tension.

Because so many of us have missed out on the first two spiritual rites of birth and puberty, sex often ends up being a poor imitation of genuine intimacy. Our relationships may become about conquering and manipulating rather than connecting and surrendering to passion. Sleeping with someone before we even know how to spell their last name has become a common practice as we crave connection yet fear intimacy.

Humans are the only animals that make the logical association between mating and reproduction. Animals are driven by instinct to breed, yet many species seem to mate for the sheer pleasure and sensation of the act. For example, the females of some bird species will invite males to mate with them even though they have already laid their eggs. Biologists have read a lot into this behavior, believing it is a trick to fool males into caring for hatchlings that they did not father. But this may be simply humans reading meaning into animal behavior. Masturbation, another sexual behavior that is divorced from reproduction, is also observed throughout the animal world. Even horses that have been castrated engage in regular self-stimulation. Scientists have yet to fully understand the mysteries of sex in its origins in the animal world.

Humans, though, appear to be the only species that can be easily sexually traumatized. Being the object of someone's lust can cause a fear of intimacy. People who were sexually abused at a young age will sometimes "act out" sexually later on, in an unconscious effort to reclaim their power. For example, they might pride themselves on being excellent at giving oral sex, secretly cheat on their partners, or engage in behaviors that are sadomasochistic—all to regain a sense of control over their sexuality.

No matter what kind of "first time" we've had, we can have a rewarding sexual encounter with our present beloved as if for the first time. Without fearing rejection or being embarrassed by our lack of skills, we can practice simply staring into each other's eyes and gently touching and kissing, focusing on intimacy rather than intercourse. And by all means avoid "make-up" sex after an argument, which may reconnect two people but can also be an excuse to avoid resolving a major conflict.

Chimpanzees show amazing displays of intimacy toward each other, but seldom when they're copulating. Humans have taken on the task of bringing intimacy, caring, vulnerability, and surrender to our mating. Our brain is programmed to crave the intense experience of orgasm because it's a fail-safe mechanism designed to ensure our species' survival. Shamans believe that the energies of love can help them enter higher states of consciousness, as do tantric practitioners who focus on directing the current of sexual ecstasy up the spine, through the chakras, and into the head, in the process awakening the higher brain. In the ecstasy of sex, shamans believe, lies a transcendence that is the closest experience to death one can have in life. After this symbolic death of the individual as a separate self, one discovers a "we" that is greater than the sum of its parts. As the poet Rumi says to his beloved, "For I have ceased to exist, only you are here." You cease to exist as a separate, disconnected individual and surrender to the bliss of communion.

An orgasm involves a dissolution of "me" and a merging into "us" as the ego steps aside. In fact, the French term for orgasm, *le petit mort,* translates as "the little death." In that blissful moment of climax, we die to our personal stories and surrender to our partner and to Spirit.

When we achieve a rapport with a sexual partner that is based on the desire to share pleasure and exploration, we can carry that dynamic of sharing into our experiences outside of the bedroom. The experience of mutual pleasure awakens the bliss centers in the brain, and open us up to joy, love, and mystical experiences. Among the brain regions activated during orgasm are the amygdala and the hypothalamus, which produces oxytocin, the so-called love and bonding hormone. Oxytocin levels jump fourfold during orgasm.

When we feel a certain chemistry with a partner, we are convinced that he or she is "the one." However, usually the person we're deeply attracted to is holding a mirror to the emotional dramas we've yet to work out. Often when we're strongly attracted to someone, it's not just a play of hormones; we are intuitively drawn to partners who we believe will help us work out emotional issues we may not be aware of yet. A soulmate provides us with an excellent opportunity to resolve these issues at last; but while our mates can *help* us heal, they cannot do the actual healing for us. If we choose to grow through our initiation, and learn our lessons, we won't remain stuck in the wrong relationship, one that simply repeats the same old emotional dramas. Our relationship becomes the right one, and we become the right partner, instead of continually searching for the right person.

In a culture dominated by masculine values, both men and women have been ignoring the feminine energies required by this rite of passage. The feminine principle honors communion instead of domination. We no longer focus on concerns such as: "What can I get from this person? Is he useful to me? Does he fit into my scheme of how to create a family or a home?" Our relationships no longer become like business transactions. We yield to mutual giving, exploration, and discovery, so our interactions become fluid, like the movements of dancers undulating around a holy fire. We must be willing to welcome the "little death," knowing that it releases us into true life. You can't have a great orgasm without a little part of you dying to the greater whole. From my counseling work I've come to believe that many men are terrified of the loss of control that orgasm represents, so that they will ejaculate simply to avoid orgasm. For a long time we have equated these two functions, but ejaculation is a physiological release localized in the male genital area, whereas the orgasm, according to neurologist Martin Portner, requires a letting go of inhibition in which the brain center associated with control and vigilance shuts down.[13]

The rite of the first sexual experience has implications that extend beyond sex. It is about approaching other people with trust, and a willingness to stretch the imagination beyond its ordinary limits. But with the experience of merging and orgasm comes the acute awareness of mortality. In that moment of surrender to your partner, you may become aware, perhaps for the first time, that you can die to your limited, separate self.

The first three initiations allow us to interact with others in harmonious, loving, and creative ways instead of perceiving them as potential enemies or pawns in a battle for survival. The next set of initiations requires that we transcend our personal identity by entering into unions in which we relinquish that very sense of self we have been developing and whose transcendence we tasted when merging with another.

CHAPTER 10

The Initiations of Maturity

For 20 years, I traveled the Andes and the Amazon, studying the wisdom teachings of the Americas. In the early days, I accompanied my Indian mentor and friend through the Altiplano, the highland plains that extend from Machu Picchu to Lake Titicaca. Later, as he grew old, my friend directed my research journeys as I trekked solo to work with the last of the living shamans.

"You'd better travel alone," he said to me once. "You know too little to teach anyone and too much to have a bad companion."

Together, we studied the research from my travels and set out to reweave the tapestry of an ancient tradition that had been torn to shreds by the Conquistadors. All we found at the beginning were the frayed ends. We rewove a bit of knowledge here and there with a snip of wisdom from another village and with the tales left by the Spanish chroniclers. Then we struck gold. We discovered that the wisdom teachings in their entirety had remained intact and were available to those who underwent the great initiation—the final one, the initiation of death.

"Where can I learn these teachings?" I asked the old Indian.

"In the Amazon," he said. "You must go back to the Garden."

Soon after, he passed away. His last words to me were, "Now your time has come to bring others to where I have taken you."

Damn. I am so angry. Why did he have to die now? He and I were the only ones who knew how little I know. . . .

Journal
Machu Picchu, Peru

The first three initiations qualify us for membership within the global village as healthy individuals. With a nascent sense of self, we leave the confines of the home to explore the larger world and take our place in it. Next, with the initiations of marriage, parenthood, and sagehood, we master the emotional forces that underlie these stages of life, ultimately preparing ourselves to meet death without fear, resistance, or denial.

The Rite of Marriage: Courage Conquering Sloth

The sacred view of marriage is found in every culture. The *hieros gamos* was the mystical union between a god and goddess, ritually reenacted by priests and priestesses in ancient Greek temples. An even earlier version of the sacred marriage comes from Sumer, a civilization in southern Iraq from around the 6th century B.C., in which the king consummated his union with the high priestess of Inanna, goddess of love and fertility. This ritual union, which occurred in the spring, served a practical purpose too, for the common folk took it as an invitation to mate, ensuring that their offspring would be born in the early winter, when they had more time to tend to them. The notion of sacred marriage exists also in Christianity, implying a union between oneself and God. This union of an invisible being and a mortal could also produce offspring, as in the "annunciation" of Mary by an angel which resulted in the birth of Christ.

Our modern idea of marriage carries some of the exalted status of the sacred marriage, while also straining under the pressure of extraordinary expectations. On the practical side, we want it to be a legal arrangement with full protection for both partners in case of dissolution. Emotionally, we want a safe place to experience our vulnerability, and we hope for romance and passionate sex for years to come (even after children arrive and wreak havoc on privacy and sleep cycles). We want our partner to offer the same acceptance as a best friend who is familiar with our every quirk and bad habit. The reality of marriage can be incredibly disillusioning when all we ever thought we wanted was to have a big party and then live happily ever after. The fear of intimacy, which we didn't overcome on our superficial passage into the rite of first love, now paralyzes us. But since there's someone else in the picture now, we figure we can let them work out how to keep the partnership alive. Then, if it doesn't succeed, we can blame them and continue our search for the perfect partner. The ego certainly has a well-constructed belief system to justify its sloth.

"Marriage" used to be a simple matter in which man-the-hunter exchanged iron-rich meat for sex provided by the woman. It was very clear what each partner brought to the table. No meat, no sex. No sex? The disgruntled hunter found another female willing to make the exchange. This barter system worked well enough to allow *Homo sapiens* to increase the population exponentially. Later, marriage was a brokered contract designed to bring warring tribes into a state of truce or bind important families to each other as two young people were married in sacrifice to the needs of the larger group. Both spouses knew what their respective duties were.

Today, women hunt for their own meat, and it's corporations, not kings, that control the wealth of nations. In Western nations, nearly half of marriages end up in divorce. But while divorce rates have multiplied, more people are getting married a second and third time. Marriage has never enjoyed such popularity! Yet what we're supposed to provide to each other is unclear. Everyone has different expectations, and the fear of disappointing, and being disappointed, paralyzes us. If only the moment of perfect joy could be frozen in time so that we could avoid making any mistakes or getting hurt.

Marriage is the passage from belonging only to one's self to becoming part of a union and committing to a great journey together. In a partnership, "being married" entails creating a primary loyalty that can become a container for a family, whether or not that family ever includes children. Two people who are never going to raise children together can come together in partnership and create an entity that provides an arena for their personal growth even as the partnership itself flourishes.

The family is the basic unit of society, and everyone conducts rites of marriage, from villagers in the Brazilian Amazon to cosmopolitan New Yorkers. But marriage has not always been an act between consenting adults. Despite reform efforts, the practice of marrying off a child bride against her will is still widely practiced in India. In European history, marriage was a business contract between two families that arranged for the betrothal of their children. In the 12th century, as Europe was going through a mini-renaissance, it was believed that marriage and love were incompatible and that love could be found only in secret trysts and affairs. Associating love with marriage is a relatively recent phenomenon in the West.

Despite the often fantastic nature of Greek myths, the marriage of Zeus and Hera sheds some light on what can go wrong in a marriage. Hera was the goddess of childbirth and creator of the entire world, as well as being the older sister of Zeus, the king of the gods and lord of the sky and thunder. Hera's temples and her cult are far more ancient than those of Zeus, but when he begins to overtake her in importance, he forces her to become his wife. Hera is unhappy with Zeus running around and seducing women (and men), and she refuses to sleep with him, thereafter becoming known among a predominantly male priesthood as the "bitch goddess."

Marriage could be a bloody and violent affair in ancient times. According to Roman legend, Romulus, the founder of Rome, sought wives for his sons in order to expand the city's population. After failing to find willing brides among the neighboring Sabines, Romulus invited them to a great feast. At the end of the celebration, the Romans slew the men and abducted the women. (The "rape of the Sabine women" became a popular subject for painters of the Renaissance.) In real life as well as in legend, it was common for conquering armies to steal the women of a vanquished nation.

The modern marriage eventually became a vehicle for personal growth. We invest our energy into the partnership in the belief that each individual will give it his or her all. If the man has not completed his initiation into first love, he will soon tire of the effort and go back to hanging out with his buddies or pursuing other women, as Zeus did. The woman, frustrated at her man's immaturity, is then belittled as the complaining "bitch."

The emotional bond between partners can be so powerful that long-parted lovers can feel the sparks of passion almost instantly upon meeting again years later. Sometimes that passion is positive, as when high school sweethearts meet again in the senior housing complex and pick up where they left off. In other cases, the lovers are still furious with each other and fall right back into the same old arguments they were having 30 years before. When that happens, it's a sure sign that the two partners failed to complete the initiation of marriage.

Many people skip the initiation altogether and remain immature youths as they enter marriage or, worse, parenthood without accepting the new role demanded of them. We see this in a man who, at the birth of his first child, feels abandoned by his wife and complains, "As soon as the baby came, there went the sex, the relationship, and the intimacy." Rather than make an effort to rekindle sexual passion and share the child care with the exhausted young mother, the new father becomes slothful and resentful. Their child becomes the target of his blame as well.

The four stages of any initiation apply to this rite just as they do to any other. When I first got married, I was so impressed with myself every time I referred to "my wife" in conversation. Being married was a badge of honor. Having a wife meant I was an adult who was wanted, exclusively, by someone—making me a very important person. This was the stage of embracing my identity as "partner" and the beginning of my initiation.

Next comes the great departure: "after the honeymoon." When the wedding dress has been stored in the dry cleaner's box, the white-lace-covered photo album placed on the shelf, and that idiot you married overdrew the checking account again, you enter this stage. You can become wistful for your bachelor or bachelorette days. If you have an affair, or revert to poker nights out with the boys, or continue confiding your deepest feelings to your old girlfriends, you get stuck in the threshold of this passage. Men have an especially hard time integrating their new state with the old warrior identity that is still central to their self-image. For example, a husband may struggle to maintain his sense of masculine independence and competence when his wife calls to ask why he's late again and why he forgot to mail the mortgage check. I remember when I reached this stage in my marriage. I had left home to lead a month's expedition to the Amazon, without paying the gas and electric utility bill. The day after I left, the power was turned off, and my wife and son were stranded at home without any heat during the first snowfall of the year. The next time I called home, my wife let me know all about it in great detail, including how irresponsibly I was behaving. And she was absolutely right. My warrior self insisted that I could simply stay in the jungle, where I had no obligations.

In the rite of marriage, integrating your old single self with your new partnered self and taking the plunge into deep intimacy are the tests you face. For me, this meant not walking out of the room when confronted with the evidence that I screwed up. It also means not threatening to leave just because you're feeling bored or restless, or because you think there might be someone better out there for you. Kahlil Gibran described the healthy meeting of these challenges of partnership this way:

> And stand together yet not too near together:
> For the pillars of the temple stand apart,
> And the oak tree and the cypress grow
> not in each other's shadow.[14]

You then move easily from having an intimate discussion with your partner, to taking time for yourself, to an evening with the old gang from your single days. In this stage, you lose all fear of what might happen if you were no longer married. The anxious thought "I don't want to be single in my 40s and have to start dating again" is no longer what keeps you in partnership.

In the final stage, illumination, you discover you're no longer defined by your marital status. You have made the alchemical union, or *coniunctio*, and crafted the philosopher's stone, known to the Greeks as *chrysopoeia*—literally, making gold. The *chrysopoeia* was the elixir of life, of immortality. The looming death that you tasted with the initiation of first love now leads to the "forever after" you discover within a sacred union. This happened to me when I was able to share every moment with my beloved, even when we were apart. It was as if the two of us had become "one flesh" and thus felt our presence in each other's hearts.

Once you've reached the stage of illumination, you have completed the initiation of marriage. Then, even if the partnership does eventually dissolve, it will be easier to let go and transition into belonging to yourself as a single person again. Anyone who's been divorced knows how much it can feel like a personal failure. In fact, divorce can be its own initiatory rite. Our culture has no guide for how to divorce in a way that leads to growth and healing for both partners. But, if you're undergoing a breakup, realize that you can revise what this initiation looks like, using it as an opportunity to do the healing you've been avoiding.

The Rite of Parenthood: Compassion Conquering Envy

We have few positive role models of parents in Western mythology. In Greek literature, we discover that Hercules kills his children in a fit of rage induced by his stepmother, Hera, that Aphrodite is born from the severed testicles of her father, Cronus, and that Psyche is sent to her fate by her tyrannical father. The Old Testament, if interpreted literally, leaves many people with the impression that God the Father is only interested in having his children pay homage to him and periodically orders his angels to destroy his offspring when they offend him, as with Sodom and Gomorrah. And Adam and Eve were such failures at parenting that their son Cain killed his brother Abel. As a result, many of us are left to discover the art of parenting on our own.

A few years ago I bought a Volvo, and when the salesperson asked, "Do you want to order leather seats?" I said, "No, I'll take naugahyde, vinyl, whatever you call it." I think he was shocked that I would want plastic seats, but as the father of two grade-school children, I could just imagine their soda pop, juice, and gum melting into the leather in the hot summer sun. My desire to maintain my image as a man in his prime, too earthy and stylish to let his skin touch synthetics, took a backseat to the reality of parenthood. If I couldn't clean the car out with a garden hose, I didn't want it. In this utilitarian vehicle I would hardly be the envy of my peers, but then I had no need to be the man with the best car on the block.

Not everyone is cut out to be or wants to be a literal parent; although we may well feel the biological urge to procreate. If we haven't undergone all our initiations up to this point, parenthood can be intensely unsettling. If our own parents got stuck at the threshold and never successfully completed this initiation, they may have passed on to us the curse of being unable to rise to the challenges of this passage. This was the case with my father, who was a wonderful partner and husband to my mother but who never discovered how to be a parent. He tried very hard, but he was a warrior and an entrepreneur who could not bring himself to hold his own grandchildren for fear they would drool on him. For a long time I was upset with my father, and my relationship with him was challenging until I became a parent myself and was faced with going through this initiation that men in our culture are so ill prepared for.

Two weeks before my son was born, I went to the infant section of a large department store and bought all the strollers and playpens and technology that I thought would make me a good parent. As I was paying the cashier, I started laughing with the realization that I could not buy enough gadgets to become a good father. My son would teach me to do that, if I allowed him. A deeply buried instinct within me rose to the surface and took over. Whatever this child needed, I would provide, no matter the cost—at least, that was my gut response. My conviction did waver many times, as it does for every parent, particularly as my son became an adolescent, but I experienced a fundamental realization that from that point on, this small person's needs would come before my own.

The father who can set aside his own needs and attend to those of his child or the mother who can cut the symbolic umbilical cord, is the parent who has had his or her initiation at the deep level of the soul. This person is ready to parent rather than just have a baby. His fears and insecurities have been healed to the point that he can enjoy his child's freedom and easy laughter without resenting that his own childhood is now truly over. When a woman says, "I want to have a baby," she may be saying, "I'm ready to make a child the focus of my life and engage in creative parenting as I discover the possibilities in the role of mother." Or she may be saying, "I'm feeling a biological urge to give birth, and I want to have a perfect infant that's a reflection of me."

Again, it's important not to see these rites only as biological passages. Even those who don't become literal parents have the opportunity at some point to mentor another person or parent an important cause or project. The same emotional issues apply. Biological parenthood means accepting a certain destiny, saying, "Yes, I will give of my body and life force to bring forth this child. Pregnancy isn't something that accidentally happened to me, and I won't bring a child into this world in order to cement a relationship." You do the same thing when you start a project. You solidify your partnership with another (because no project comes about without help), and then fashion a container to hold your delicate new "baby" before it arrives. You recognize that otherwise the "baby" will suffer and that you must nourish and protect it. You can assess the genuine needs of your endeavor, and you don't resent the hard work you have to put into it.

Planting a seed, beginning a project, is easy, but you have to tend it carefully so that your "children" have a safe and secure grounding. A child in an unstable situation will look outside the family for the structure and rules he needs. Sociologists have found that gangs often take the place of extended family, replacing them by providing strict rules about loyalty, conformity, and hierarchy. A metaphorical family, like a musical group or a charitable project, also needs a strong foundation to support it. The idea of giving birth to a child and caring for its practical needs is an organic metaphor for just about any enterprise. You sweat, prepare, hone, craft, and prune. You start with passion, you become pregnant, you carry the idea with you, and you feed it with your life force. If your life force is being directed to sustaining yourself only, you can't create anything. Biology shuts down your fertility if you're starving. Emotional dramas use up all the nourishment that a book project, a building project, or a new venture needs, and it withers up and dies. But if you take your place as a team player, negotiating and compromising without violating your integrity, you'll put the project's need ahead of your own when that's required.

Parents, Children, and Sacrifices

To better understand illumined parenting, let me describe the rather harsh history of human parenting. Society didn't always perceive children the way we do now, as special beings quite different from adults and deserving of exceptional, nurturing treatment. In hunter-gatherer societies, children didn't add great value to the tribe, because it was very difficult to outrun a predator or travel long distances with an infant at one's side. The women of the tribe used herbs to prevent conception and taught new mothers to extend their breast-feeding after giving birth, so as to postpone fertility and limit the number of babies they bore. In agricultural societies, children quickly became valuable because they could begin farming or herding at an early age, but this was their only value. Women in developing countries still give birth to many children, even if there are few resources to sustain their brood, in the hope that a few will survive long enough to care for their elders and tend the fields. They don't wonder, "Will my son feel jealous if I have another child?" Young children in these families don't spend their time playing; they take care of their younger siblings and cousins, leaving the stronger, more agile ones to be productive in the fields. By the age of seven a child would be tending the herd. Our ideas about a child being something very different from a miniature adult, and childhood being a privileged time for play, learning, and development, requiring complete parental dedication, are very recent.

One of my students is a ranger at a national park in Ethiopia, and as part of her job she runs an urgent-care clinic. One of her patients was a boy from a nearby village who was accidentally shot in the leg, which became gangrenous. The doctors proposed amputating the limb to save child's life, and my friend offered to pay for the operation. The mother, who lived in poverty, responded in a way that seems raw and cruel to us, but which was very pragmatic to her: "What use will he be to me with only one leg? Let him die and join his other two brothers who passed away during birth." Fortunately, my friend is a gifted healer, and she spent many months cleaning the infected limb. Today the boy is alive and well.

If you don't complete your initiation into parenthood, you feel the main purpose of your progeny is to add to your own survival and security. Instead of sacrificing for them, you wait for the day when they will start paying you back. You become willing to shortchange your projects the minute you feel overburdened and they stop reaping big rewards. Or you may start too many ventures, not really nurturing any of them properly. Your "children" suffer, because you don't have the energy and focus needed to care for each of them.

A parent who is stunted in his own growth may project his lost dreams on to his son and demand that the boy be the football hero his father never was or ridicule him for not being athletic.

The rite of parenting, like all initiations, involves overcoming one of our seven demons—in this case it is envy. When you're comfortable with who you are and what you have, you can dedicate yourself fully to your offspring and help them recognize their gifts.

The Rite of Sagehood: Temperance Conquering Gluttony

Among African wildebeests, older males are driven out of the herd by the younger, more fertile, and stronger males, ensuring that the herd's progeny carry the genes of the hardiest members. When survival is foremost, old and weak animals are cast aside in favor of the young. However, human beings have discovered that sheer strength and the ability to procreate are not the only attributes that help us to thrive. As we accept the decline of our fertility or potency, we can embrace a new power: wisdom. For humans, survival is not only of the fittest but also of the wisest.

You don't have to wait until you are an old man or woman to become wise. When a new baby arrives, she displaces the older sibling as the parents' attentions focus on the newborn. Like the old wildebeest, the older child observes longingly as the mother cuddles the younger one. He must develop a certain wisdom at this young age or else he is likely to act out angrily for the rest of his life.

Our culture worships the ideal of perpetual youth, so we fight the passage into the stages of elder and sage. *Puer aeternus* is a Latin term for "eternal boy" that psychologists have used to describe a man who is unable or unwilling to grow up and remains tied to his mother throughout his life. Michael Jackson was a living example of this archetype and even admitted that he identified with the character Peter Pan, the boy who never grew up. Paris Hilton's persona might be seen as the feminine equivalent, the eternal girl, or *puella aeterna*. What a contrast these cultural models of behavior are to the Inuit elder who recognized that the best way to ensure the tribe's survival was to walk out onto an ice floe and calmly wait for death to take him away.

A materialistic culture doesn't seem to have much use for the sage's wisdom. The history of the clan or the perspective that comes from years of living and working the land is no longer valued. People tend to be more interested in what the latest gorgeous, 20-something celebrity has to say about the meaning of life. But it is the sage, like the innocent child, who can foresee opportunities when everyone else sees problems. Our greatest sages of late have not been the elders, since seniors have been riveted by protecting their jobs or their retirement, but rather the young visionaries who launched wildly successful computer and Internet enterprises. They discerned the change from brick and mortar to virtual, and from the information age to a new wisdom society.

We have all met precocious children who seem so much wiser than their parents. A youthful visionary of history was Saint Joan of Arc, a peasant girl who led the French armies in several stunning and decisive victories against the English during the Hundred Years' War. Joan was only 18 in 1430 when she was sent by King Charles VII to the siege at Orléans as part of a relief mission. Within days of her arrival she gained the respect of the hardened military commanders who, following her tactics, managed to end the siege in nine days. Because she claimed she was being guided by God, Joan was burned at the stake for being a heretic, yet later the same Church canonized her as a saint. Although perceptions about aging are changing in America as the large baby-boomer population resists the old stereotypes about growing older, middle age still means recognizing that you're no longer the coveted advertising demographic because no one cares all that much what brands you're buying. It means the music of your youth that felt so rebellious and fresh is now played on the oldies station along with low-budget ads for pain relievers.

The man who completes the initiation into sagehood no longer sees younger men as competition and begins to mentor them. He transitions from being the handsome young prince and steps gracefully into his kingly role. He does not become an angry, bitter old man, and he is able to forge partnerships with others with tolerance and admiration for those who are younger, faster, and more vital. He doesn't hide his weaknesses behind the diamond-studded Rolex or the high-maintenance mistress. The woman embracing this stage of life no longer plays the pouting princess. Princesses don't age well. They have to become queenly—and avoid becoming evil queens or drama queens conniving to amass power, influence, and material wealth.

The feminine sage doesn't replace the earlier roles of maiden and mother; she transcends and includes them. She has integrated her identities. The sage is her own woman while serving as a valuable contributor to a community and a partnership; she's a mother, a sexually active and sensual maiden, and a grandmother who has transcended the limitations of all the roles she's played in her life.

Although she can no longer give birth physically, she continues to bring forth and nurture what is of value to her and to others.

Similarly, a man can integrate the best qualities of his youth into a new identity as the sage, if he has the courage to complete this initiation rather than simply going through the motions of aging more gracefully. A friend of mine from the World War II generation keeps his hand in various business projects because, as he says, he's good at the game of business and enjoys it. He engages in service projects that appeal to his interests, and he makes time for his personal life, which includes his wife, sons, grandchildren, and friends. He's clear about what he wants to do and doesn't waver in his dedication to spending his later years exactly as he wants to spend them. What's more, he inspires younger people— whether he's teaching them about how to work efficiently within a nonprofit organization or taking off with his wife on a bike tour in a remote part of Asia.

My friend knows that the loss of fertility doesn't have to be a metaphorical loss of self-worth as well. He knows that it's okay to forgo the bingo games and head straight for a hiking adventure. As sages, we don't resign ourselves to being outcasts and discards. During my travels through the high mountains of the Andes, I learned that people traditionally entered this stage at age 40, because they didn't live long after that. Today, we're redefining aging and doing in our 70s what our grandparents did in their 40s and 50s. If we can open our eyes to the initiation of sagehood, we can discover all the ways in which we can contribute to our world instead of focusing on gathering as much wealth as possible to cure our discomfort with growing old.

Sagehood requires continually rediscovering our value while accepting that we aren't the sum of our accomplishments, that we may have gifts to offer that are simple—and sometimes not likely to earn us much attention—but important nonetheless.

One of the advantages of remaining physically, mentally, and socially active as we get older is that we recognize that we have a modicum of control over the aging process. This alleviates some of the fear that seizes us when we realize that our next initiation will be the final one of our lives.

The Rite of the Great Crossing: Humility Conquering Pride

Shamans in traditional societies believe that to conquer the fear of death, one must experience it *mythically*. In some cultures, an initiate might be buried in the sand for several days with only a straw in his mouth to breathe through. In the Amazon, he might ingest ayahuasca, a powerful hallucinogenic concoction designed to induce an altered state of consciousness, in which he will practice facing his death symbolically. I remember the first time I experienced this jungle brew. After I got over the nausea and had purged several times through every opening in my body, I smelled a putrid odor. I turned to my right and saw that my arm was decomposing and there were worms and maggots crawling through my flesh. I tried to scream for help, but I could not utter a sound. My mouth no longer responded to me. I was terrified as my body continued rotting before me with an overwhelming stench, until all the flesh was gone, leaving behind only the whitened bones of my skeleton. I remember thinking to myself, "Well, I am dead already, this is the worst that can happen." But I was wrong.

Next, I began to see images of all the suffering that humans have inflicted on each other throughout history. It was as if I were watching a movie that I couldn't stop, and experiencing all the feelings and sensations of every wretched act I witnessed. I had not yet learned that one can guide these experiences, literally changing channels, and I was stuck watching the channel that replayed all the atrocities people had ever committed against their fellow men and women. And then it all stopped, and there was only the night sky and a beautiful emptiness, and I heard a voice telling me that I had always existed, since before time began, and that while this was the history of humanity, it did not need to be my story. Then the voice showed me how time began, in a vivid replay of what I imagine the Big Bang of creation must have looked like. Afterward, I glanced down and saw that my body was whole once again. I was exhausted but in bliss. I had been shown that death is only a doorway into eternity and understood why this was called the great initiation.

The goal of shamanic practices like these is to decouple our consciousness from our physical body so that we can identify with a self that is eternal. In fact, in order to maintain their perspective of eternity in light of the enduring illusion that the world of the flesh is all there is, shamans regularly revisit experiences such as the one that I had in the Amazon. After the first few times, they no longer need to go through the agonizing death of their physical body, and they pop straight through into an illumined state. Then, when the moment of physical death arrives, they make the great crossing easily, without fear, as they already know the way back home.

Death can feel like the ultimate encounter with terror. You may have tasted this fear when someone died in your presence —whether it was a loved one, a person you admired from afar, or a stranger who perished in a car accident whose body you saw covered up and lying on the road as you and the other commuters drove soberly past the scene. At such moments, the mechanism of denial breaks down and we remember our mortality.

Conquering the fear of death allows us to experience our power even as we're humbled by how small we are in the greater scheme of things. It lets us dream big, even if we still have to get up at the crack of dawn every day and attend to a long list of labors before our head hits the pillow again. It's what allows us to go forth with a sense of purpose, knowing that if this were our last day on earth, we would have spent it well. It's what gives us the strength to simply smile when someone underestimates us and feel no need to prove them wrong. We reserve our energy for doing what matters to us, not for convincing the world that we're very important.

When this is our way of living, death becomes a natural process. We don't violently resist or hold on to the last breath. Our pride dissolves because we realize how small we are, and we're humbled by our role in Creation. Fear gives way to awe and trust.

When we experience the great crossing in this manner, we don't postpone it to the last days of our life.

Those last moments as we lie on our deathbed, saying goodbye to everyone and everything that we love, are not the best times to experience this initiation. There's too much going on for us to be able to fully relish the freedom and grace that it bestows upon us. The shaman knows that this initiation is best experienced mythically in preparation for the end of life on this earth.

Initiation and Resurrection

In the West, our most poignant story of death and resurrection is that of Jesus. He taught that we can be reborn into a life in which we identify with the spirit, not the flesh. But while physical resurrection is the stuff of myth and legend, spiritual resurrection is common to all initiations and isn't supposed to be a one-time occurrence in our lives. Anytime we undergo an initiation, we experience a death of our previous identity. When we come through the other side, it's as if we were a new creature, emerging gloriously from the primordial ooze that was our former life. Shaking off the muck and the fear, we turn our face to the sun and move forward boldly in our new skin. After the initiation of death, we no longer identify with the circumstances that used to seem so very important. The new self has a wisdom the old self lacked. When you are resurrected, you realize you have a sacred power to participate in making your world a paradise.

Resurrection involves reclaiming our birthright to live in joy and optimism. Much of the time, our world seems not at all heavenly, and given all we know and have seen, it's difficult to let go of our cynicism and return to a childlike state of innocence. If we don't complete an initiation, we can't be reborn because we haven't yet died. The best we can do is make superficial changes in our lives, patching and reinventing ourselves.

It's not easy to go from caterpillar to butterfly, and the first few flights can be a little scary. If you settle for mere reinvention, you'll soon see that you're wearing the same old caterpillar shell of "overworked and underappreciated," or "wife who is now divorced but still married to the idea that she can't be complete without a man." With courage, however, you can come out on the other side, able to reclaim your right to wisdom and power. If you haven't shifted into identifying with your immortal self, that wisdom and power will be limited, just as your mortal self is limited. Your wisdom will be about the workings of the world, not about the workings of Spirit. But if you see that you're an essential, indispensable part of Creation, you understand that you're responsible for creating your experience in this life. You'll stop believing that creation happens from the top down, with an all-wise supernatural being directing traffic on those rare occasions when he feels like getting involved in the world. Instead, you'll understand that you're essential for the creative process and that Spirit is looking to you for input and direction.

The next task for the shaman is to gather her personal power, so that she can draw upon it to create. She must remain awake, remembering what she learned when she tasted immortality.

CHAPTER 11

The Shaman's Gifts: Building Personal Power

"*And the secret?*" I asked as he lowered his eyes to meet mine across the fire.

"*The secret follows from mastery of invisibility and of time. It is not the secret that is important; it is our ability to keep this secret, it is how we hold it. Knowing it is like knowing the future, and who but those that understand that time turns like a wheel can manage to know the future and not let it upset their balance? If your faith in reality is based on a belief that time moves in one direction only, then the foundations of your faith will be shattered by an experience of the future. This does not concern the shaman, because the shaman has no need for faith—the shaman has experience. Nevertheless, it takes great skill to know the future and not allow your knowledge to spoil your actions or your intent.*

"*Those who are buried here know such things. They slipped through time, and tasted our destiny.*"

Island of the Sun
Alberto Villoldo and Erik Jendresen

The shaman develops three gifts that are acquired during the course of her initiations. Together they help her to break free of the notion of linear, clock time and the fear that it will run out, and to experience her immortality. The prehistoric brain only understands today, not the future. It operates only in present tense. The new brain comprehends past and future, including the kind of time described by quantum physics, which pretzels and wormholes backward and forward on itself. In the shamanic traditions, this experience of time is referred to as infinity.

The three gifts are: the Gift of Audacity, the Gift of Patience, and the Gift of Discernment.

These gifts allow you to transcend the world of predators and prey, where time is a precious commodity that is always running short. They provide you all the time in the world and grant you the freedom to stop worrying about running out of time. They keep you from becoming lost in the dramas and traumas of the past or the unrealized dreams of the future. They bring fully online the gifts of the neocortex.

The Gift of Audacity

For an acorn to germinate, it must burst forth from its husk. The seedling has limited nourishment to fuel its growth as it starts pushing upward toward the sunlight. But it can't see the sun from its place underground, so it trusts that it will find the sun's life-giving energy at just the right moment. It doesn't remain within the hull, saying to itself, "There isn't much water this spring, so I'd better wait for next year. Who knows what will happen to the great oak within me if I blow my one chance?"

To be audacious, you must act. All the good intentions in the world and all the deepest spiritual revelations and insights are useless if you remain in the comfort of the womb, the safety of the college classroom, or the familiarity of a dead relationship, hoping that at some point you'll have enough confidence to enter the big world. You also have to let go of the illusion that all action is equally effective. We can create a lot of mindless busywork for ourselves. Not long ago, I met a woman who was exhausted by her life and frustrated by all she had to do. When we went to her house for lunch, I found it was immaculate: not a fingerprint marred the shiny surface of her appliances or granite counter, and everything was perfectly organized and spotless. The energy that she was putting into keeping order in her home was energy she could have used to be more innovative and daring. The more she polished and perfected her space, the less she was available to act creatively. You can polish your résumé, your countertops, or your halo, but none of it matters if you don't walk out the door into a creative life.

I've also met people who have read hundreds of self-help books and attended countless seminars over the years but who struggle with the same problems they've had since childhood. Their great effort at personal growth has become an addiction. They act, but not audaciously. Spending time talking about a problem, imagining how to work through it, and fretting about its existence provides the illusion of movement, but it doesn't propel you into other possibilities. You can't scheme your way into genuine creativity. You can only invite its generative force into your life and enjoy being clueless about what's coming next.

The practice of audacity requires that we give up our endless ruminating about what might happen if we act, and instead simply follow our instinct, like the acorn reaching for the sunlight. Not being able to predict the exact outcome of our action, we boldly move forward anyway, excited and eager to see what we'll bring about. We embrace our role as artists, knowing that we're not the only one with a paintbrush, and that life has its own ideas to contribute.

Many artists will say that the best works they've ever created were ones that seemed to take off on their own, to spring forth from their pen or brush. They're describing the type of creativity that occurs when you let go of your concerns about the final product. Upon closer examination, every truly innovative action seems impossibly difficult and crazy, from the construction of the Eiffel Tower, to kindergartners in America who correspond with their peers in the former Soviet Union during the 1970s to foster world peace. If an action looks comfortably familiar but packaged in a new skin labeled "new and improved," it is likely to lead you back to the same situations that weren't working for you.

Practicing audacity awakens you from the nightmare of a faulty childhood, when you longed to have the same toys everyone else had; out of the trance of prolonged youth, when you had to dress and be like everyone else; out of the delusion of flawed intimacy, where you thought your relationship had to be the perfect courtship forever; out of the chimera of imperfect parenthood, where you're ruled by your children's whims and striving to be the perfect mom or dad. If you don't awaken, you get stuck endlessly staring at your reflection by the pool, obsessed with bettering yourself but too scared to make more than superficial changes.

Most of us have forgotten how to approach life audaciously. We learned to conform at an early age, remembering the art teacher who walked around our third-grade classroom, took our unacceptably lopsided clay creation, and crushed it into a compact ball, saying, "Try again next time—that wasn't worth saving." Genuine innovation can take patience and courage. Seldom do we get the instant, perfect outcome, a glorious masterpiece that appears magically, without effort, craft, or honing.

Rather than have confidence that we can create what we truly want, we put forth a token effort at reinvention and settle for a rough draft of what we desire. We become romantically involved with someone we don't like all that much or buy into a lifestyle that's completely out of sync with our values, hopes, and longings. We settle for the heavily processed "instant" version of life, thinking that if we just add a little juice, we won't notice how artificial and inadequate it is.

The shaman lives audaciously by daring to act differently again and again. She doesn't have to come up with a business plan for every move she's going to make. Instead, she lives daringly and acts with inspiration in small deeds each day, knowing that this is the way to create something truly original. We're living in a time of great challenges that call for bold, authentic, and creative responses. We must imagine life without fossil fuels or without cars. We must fathom how we might let go of the old relationships, behaviors, institutions, and systems—and dream something entirely new. Audacity requires us to question everything, even all that we know about ourselves.

Audacity is saying yes to the call to live daringly, but not stupidly, risking the security of the familiar and delving into the unknown. It means turning adjectives into verbs, so that you're not merely a "loving person," you simply *love*, fearlessly. You are no longer a "caring person," you *care*. You are no longer a "creative individual," you *create*. It means you don't wait until you have all your ducks in a row to make a splash, because you recognize that doing so will only prevent you from living courageously today. When you live without audacity, you may be very busy, but you won't move any closer to a life of originality. Small acts of courage, from confronting tension in a relationship to questioning the rules of how an institution operates, are what keep you fresh.

Audacity turns on the neocortex, the brain that allows you to perceive your timeless nature. The great awakening to infinity will make you realize that no reputation or accumulation of power, prestige, and possessions can come near the value of living with originality. It will allow you to understand and accept that there is no safety, other than within you, so there's no point in trying to fabricate it.

The Gift of Patience

The discipline of patience has nothing to do with waiting. Patience is about understanding the right moment for action and the right moment for stillness. Our confusion about action that's fruitful versus action that's futile keeps us very busy trying to work things out in our lives and our world. We have to practice audacity, but we also have to practice patience.

When you're patient, you don't squander resources and you don't become overwhelmed by your problems. You draw in every beam of sunshine to feed yourself before your leaves turn, and you don't spring from the earth too soon and get caught in an early frost. You wait for the right timing instead of trying to force matters just to create the illusion of progress.

Patience helps you to recognize that many of the most distressing situations will clear up by themselves in due time. For the shaman, patience means having trust in *mañana,* the moment that will set everything right without your having to orchestrate or micromanage the process

With all the problems facing us in our personal lives as well as on the planet, it's easy to become manic and do everything you possibly can to fix it all right now. The shaman remembers that transformation always requires death—the death of dreams, of old ways of doing things, of pride, of reputation, and of personal importance.

We are preoccupied with our own importance when we get involved in dramas that waste our time—whether it's an ugly breakup or a sniping battle of pundits who are convinced they know how to save us. The shaman lets go of his need to forcibly assert his influence on the world. Instead, he chooses to strike a balance between lightning-fast action and stillness. He knows he plays a role in dreaming a better world.

The primitive part of our brain that perceives only our time-limited existence can't stand to wait. It wants action *now.* We impatiently shake a finger at life a lot. We lecture, rant, argue, and pressure people to make a decision *right now.* We press the elevator button furiously, as if the mechanisms will magically respond to our sense of urgency. The practice of patience, of allowing *mañana*— "morning" or "tomorrow" in Spanish—to sort out the majority of our problems, gives us the energy to deal with what we actually do need to address. A friend of mine had a major project that was due in three days, and that required coordinating teams in four countries and across seven time zones. She was overwhelmed simply trying to get everyone on the phone at the same time. Then she realized she had to do her part and let the universe take care of the rest. The only way to do what needed to be done was to have clarity about what she could delegate, to someone else or to *mañana*. And everything turned out exactly as it had to.

Patience also allows us to stop obsessing over what isn't happening and appreciate the movement we see, even if it's just a trickle of motion. We feel comfortable with what we're able to do, and don't give up our dreams just because they take time to manifest and effort to make them a reality. We're glad to be able to add a few brushstrokes here and there. We don't get bogged down in planning, and don't get caught up in busywork. What needs to get done simply gets done. This is an incredibly difficult practice in a society that believes that we should pull ourselves up by our bootstraps. This is fine if you are trying to build up strength in your legs, but fruitless otherwise. Good things come to those who wait.

The Gift of Discernment

Discernment is the unemotional examination of the facts. Without discernment, we fly blind and have to rely on autopilot, responding to life from the primitive brain and its propensity for emotional judgment. Being a discerning witness allows us to observe what's happening and to be honest with ourselves and others about it. Once we see the facts unemotionally, we can set aside our beliefs so we don't have to discard the facts we don't like while playing up the importance of the ones that support our own worldview. We can then write a new story about our situation in the moment, because our vision is unclouded.

When I was in the Amazon, one day I strayed off the trail, only to discover I could not find my way back to camp. We were many hours from the nearest village, in a beautiful yet desolate region of the rainforest. After a couple of hours following animal trails, I realized I was lost and started getting afraid, as night was about to fall. But then I stopped and told myself, "You are not lost. Lost is a state of mind. You simply do not know where you are." By rephrasing the facts of my situation, I was able to avoid panicking and perhaps avoided doing something foolish. Instead,

I found a small stream and followed that to where it merged into the Amazon, and I caught a ride home on a passing indigenous canoe with a powerful outboard motor.

The discipline of discernment allows you to stop thinking about what you could have been, or what you'll be someday when you find the time, and become exactly who you are today. You recognize that you're a part of Creation unfolding and that this Creation is perfect in this very moment.

It can be very difficult to feel that your life is perfect. Even if your life is going smoothly and you're not feeling any great suffering, you're likely to look around at the world and think it's incredibly troubled and in need of immediate, major repair. Your frustration can't convince China to improve its treatment of Tibet. To actually play your part in the healing of the world, beyond putting a "Free Tibet" sticker on your car bumper, is to witness the complexity of the situation and observe how history unfolds. It repeats itself when no one's been paying close attention, but eventually—if there are concerned people involved—problems sort themselves out.

Your need to fix it all, *right now,* is rooted in an inability to experience the perfection in how things are. Pining for a huge canvas when you have several small ones in front of you at any time is no excuse for not painting. Wishing for world peace is no excuse for being inconsiderate to your neighbors. Discernment allows you to stop personalizing problems and setting yourself up to be a noble savior.

All the great wisdom traditions include the concept of an observer who doesn't identify with anything that happens but merely watches, whether he's witnessing tragedy or comedy. The image of the wise old man or woman clucking his or her tongue at human folly teaches us to stand back and see how life choreographs itself with a little help from all of us. As Lord Krishna told the reluctant warrior Arjuna in the Bhagavad Gita, we cannot succeed in life or the spiritual path by avoiding challenges and being inactive. We must play our part in life, according to our given nature, but with detachment, knowing that something greater than ourselves acts through us.

CONCLUSION

The stone had three symbols carved in it. It was old, the symbols worn smooth from fingers rubbing on them.

"It's a prayer stone," Don Antonio said. "Shamans don't pray with words, like you do. We pray by summoning the power of images."

I looked at the smooth rock in my hands and tried to imagine myself praying, but no feelings or images would come. Strange, I thought, because I had recently lost my father, my marriage had broken apart, and I had been a jumble of feelings and tears for the last few months. Yet I felt no emotions.

"I only know how to pray with words," I mumbled awkwardly.

"Then you don't know how to pray," he muttered, and looked at the horizon to where the sun was setting somewhere over the Pacific Ocean. Behind us, the snowcapped Andes glowed softly pink and orange.

"These symbols represent the three disciplines of the shaman. Keep it, it's a gift," he said.

The stone was the size and shape of a computer mouse, and it fit nicely in my palm. "Apple should make a mouse like this," I thought. Then I began berating myself for thinking of something this trivial after being gifted with an object of power by a high shaman from the Andes. "You can take the man out of the city," I sighed, "but you can't take the city out of the man."

Later that evening, I sat by the fire holding the stone. I recognized the symbols as part of the Laika, or pre-Inka, iconography that I had studied over the years. The sun, the stars, and the universe, represented by a circle with a dot in the center, the familiar five-pointed star, and arrows pointing in four directions. According to the mythology of the Laika, they were the children of the sun and had come from the stars. But what was I supposed to make of this rock in my hand?

Don Antonio looked at me across the fire. "Sleep with it and discover how to pray in the realm where the mind cannot follow, in your dreams." Without saying another word, he stood up, walked into his hut, and went to bed.

For a moment, the thought crossed my mind to simply toss the stone in the fire. I'm not good at riddles and don't like them. But I had known this man for many years, and he'd been like a father to me, teaching me everything about an ancient wisdom that the Spanish Conquistadors had nearly eradicated. These were the teachings of the Laika, shamans who had lived long before the Inka. Grudgingly, I took the stone with me into my tent and crawled into my sleeping bag. The Andean days are warm, yet as soon as the sun sets, the temperature at 14,000 feet drops precipitously. I snuggled into the down-filled bag, feeling my toes grow warm as I pressed against the hot water bottle I'd placed there earlier, my one concession to luxury at high altitude.

That night, I dreamed. I was a boy, no older than nine or ten, back in my family home in Havana, and it was Christmastime. I wasn't taught much about Santa Claus, but each sixth day of January, the day when the Three Wise Men came bearing gifts to the Child Jesus, there would be presents under the tree for all of us children. In my dream, there were the Three Kings, standing in my living room, each holding out a small chest toward me. I told them, "These are not for me." They said nothing and opened the boxes, and in each was a tablet inscribed with single word:

TODAY

TOMORROW

FOREVER

"But where is the frankincense, the myrrh, and the gold?" I cried.

I woke up while it was still dark, disturbed by the dream, waiting for the warmth of the first rays of the sun. As soon as the dawn washed over my tent, it became like an oven, and I scurried out to restart our fire and put on a pot of water. A while later, the old man came out of his hut, looked at me, and grinned.

"Why are you smiling?" I asked, then hurriedly added, "Good morning."

"You received three gifts," he replied. "The dreams never cease to amaze me." And he shook his head as he reached for the pot of boiling coffee.

Don Antonio thinks that my dream holds some kind of shamanic significance. The anthropologist in me is appalled. Why are the wise men bringing me gifts? On the one hand, I do feel like the teachings of the shamans can help me, and I seem to have been chosen by accident or fate to be a chronicler for them. But I'm no shaman. In fact, I really just want to have a good time climbing the mountains and not take any of this too seriously.

My therapist would have a field day with this dream. Then again, maybe the message is what's important. Today, tomorrow, forever.

"Let's start with tomorrow," Don Antonio said. "Mañana. For you, it's simply the day that comes after this one, clock time rolling inexorably forward. For us, mañana is a philosophy, a way of life largely misunderstood by Westerners. You use the word to describe us as lazy Indians."

He paused, reached down into the fire, and picked up a glowing ember that he dropped into his carved iron wood pipe. I had brought that pipe for him from the jungle as a gift. He drew deeply on it and blew a cloud of blue smoke toward the sun.

"For us, mañana means not doing today what will take care of itself tomorrow."

He looked sternly at me. "Mañana means trusting the implicit order of the universe, even if you cannot understand it at the moment."

"Mira," he said, "Look. The sun will rise tomorrow even if we're not here to witness it, no?" A couple of evenings earlier, I'd been telling him *about the old philosophical riddle: If a tree falls in the forest and there is no one around to hear it, does it make a sound?*

"But this concept of mañana is just a way of avoiding personal responsibility," I said.

"No," he said, shaking his head. "You do what needs to be done today, and no more. Not one inch more. You can also call it the gift of patience. This discipline is very difficult for gringos, who want everything today."

"You mean, learning to wait?" I asked.

"No, no waiting," the old man said. "You don't wait for buses, for taxis, for friends, for your luck to change. No waiting. When you're at the bus stop, you are enjoying the warm sun on your back, or the rain. But you're not waiting for the bus. Waiting will make you insane."

"But weren't you waiting for the water to boil just now so you could have a cup of coffee?"

"No, I was enjoying the warmth of the coals, and then the water boiled. I poured myself a cup, no sooner, no later." Then he added, "I never wait anymore, and everything comes to me. My own teacher learned that only as an old man, but not because he had become old, but because he'd discovered the practice of mañana, of tomorrow.

"Which brings us to today," he said. "Today annihilates yesterday. The person who went to sleep last night no longer exists. But you like to cling to the idea that you have a personal history, a past, and that this is your identity."

"But of course I have a past. I have a mother and father," I objected, "and furthermore, I went to the university and got a Ph.D. All that is a part of who I am."

"That was someone else," he answered. "Remember that stream we had to cross to reach my hut here in the mountains? Well, when we return we won't be crossing the same stream. It'll be a whole new rush of water, carrying the rains that fell this morning on the hilltops."

"You mean that we don't cross the same stream twice?" I asked, repeating the time-worn adage.

"Yes," he replied, and mulled my answer over. "In fact, you don't even cross the same stream once."

He reached for the pot of boiling water and refilled his cup.

"*The practice of today is to realize that you don't exist at all. It takes great courage to practice this. That's why it's also called the gift of audacity. Because if you don't exist, none of the things you do have any significance. And nothing terrifies men more than losing their sense of personal importance.*" *He swept his arm across the horizon to include the snowcapped peaks and the river below, "Really, none of this means anything."*

"*Not even your sacred wisdom teachings?*" *I asked, hoping to stump him, as I was still smarting from his casual dismissal of all I had accomplished, the quick waving away of my personal history.*

"*Not even the wisdom teachings,*" *he replied. "They have to be discovered anew by every generation. Otherwise, they're a lie. They are like that pile of llama shit,*" *he said, pointing behind him with his pipe. "No nourishment left."*

"*But the mountains are real, aren't they?*" *I asked.*

"*Of course, they're real,*" *he replied. "Don't ask me stupid questions."* *Then he added, "But they're real only because you perceive them to be so."*

Now I was really confused. I asked the old man to explain how they could be real but only if I perceived them as real.

"*You can think of it as waking up in the morning and looking at yourself in the mirror and being surprised.*"

"*So,*" *I said, a smile forming on my lips, "you're telling me I should look in the mirror first thing in the morning and tell myself, 'I don't know who you are, but I will shave you anyway . . .'?"*

"*Yes! Exactly.*" *He laughed and passed me the boiling water pot. "Here, have another cup of coffee."*

"*But who is drinking this coffee, if I don't exist?*" *I asked.*

"*Aha!*" *he exclaimed. "That is the perennial question that has preoccupied shamans and initiates of every spiritual discipline. Some have even turned it into a practice, repeating the question 'Who am I?' and then inquiring, 'Who is it that is asking this question?'"*

"*Sounds like a pretzel to me, like an endless loop.*"

"*Yes,*" *replied the old man. "That's what the shamans of old discovered. They found out it was more important to ask the question than to find the answer. And then they reached the inevitable conclusion that they did not exist. They perceived that they were a bundle of vibrating* strings made of light who had assembled a body for a brief measure of time. After this realization, they were free to step into forever."

I tossed out the dregs of coffee in my cup and started rummaging through my backpack for the tiny espresso coffeemaker I always traveled with. This conversation was getting too heady for me, and I needed a shot of caffeine to kick-start brain cells that were not firing properly at that altitude. I love coffee, but generally avoid it. Yet I didn't think I could follow him into "forever" without a double espresso.

I unscrewed the filter, filled the bottom half with water, and topped it with my favorite Colombian blend. I balanced the tiny aluminum pot between two stones and pushed a few embers beneath it with a branch.

I turned to the old man and asked him, "How come you've never talked to me about these three practices before?"

"Because you had never gone through your initiation," he replied.

I was confused. I had spent the previous 15 years studying with him and shamans in the Amazon and had gone through all of their rites of passage. In fact, I reminded him that I had earned the same level and degree as he had, although of course, he had many more years of experience and wisdom.

"Those rites are simply acknowledgments of your learning," he said. "Initiation is different. It is the dark night of the soul that puts you through the meat grinder of life. Initiation means coming out tempered by pain, having grown through sacrifice and courage. Like what you have gone through with the loss of your father and your family. Before, you were a boy attempting to raise a family, making the same mistakes your father made. You are a man now, and you will become a good father. There are many who fail this passage and are left crippled or wounded by it, angry at the bad turn their life has taken. Those who succeed acquire a new level of power and humility."

I understood. I closed my eyes, and to my surprise, I felt a tear slip out, moistening my sun-parched lips. I knew what he meant about my now being a father—not biologically, which anyone can become—but being a father consciously. It was a passage I had resisted, clinging to my old desire to be free, looking out on a horizon filled with possibilities for myself, unwilling to admit that this stage of my life had already slipped into the past.

"Let's leave forever for tomorrow," I said. I'd had enough teaching for the morning, and I needed some time to assimilate what the old man had said.

The old Indian reached for the espresso maker, looked up at me, and smiled. "Forever can wait," he said.

ENDNOTES

1. An archetype is a pattern of experience or behavior common to all human beings.

2. "Reset switch for brain cells discovered," *Pain & Central Nervous System Week,* November 17, 2003.

3. Don Richardson, *Peace Child,* (Seattle, WA: YWAM Publishing, 2007).

4. Phil Zuckerman at Pitzer College in Claremont, California, refers to investigations by Gregory Paul in "Why the Gods are not Winning" in *The Edge,* web edition #209, May, 2007. (See also Phil Zuckerman's book *Society without God: What the Least Religious Nations Can Tell Us About Contentment.*)

5. Richard Dawkins, *River Out of Eden: A Darwinian View of Life,* (New York: Basic Books, 1995), 131–132.

6. James Prescott, Ph.D., "Prevention or therapy and the politics of trust: inspiring a new human agenda," *Psychotherapy and Politics International,* (New York: John Wiley & Sons, Ltd., 2009) published online January 10, 2006.

7. Andrew Newberg, as reported in his book, *Why God Won't Go Away: Brain Science & the Biology of Belief.*

8. Marcus E. Pembrey, Lars Olov Bygren, Gunaar Kaati, et al. "Sex-specific, male-line transgenerational responses in humans." *European Journal of Human Genetics,* (2006), 159–166, published online December 14, 2005, http://www.nature.com/ejhg/journal/v14/n2/full/5201538a.html.

9. Georges Charbonnier, *Conversations with Claude Lévi-Strauss,* 29–30, quoted by Leonard Shlain in *The Alphabet Versus the Goddess.*

10. Bootie Cosgrove-Mather, "Poll: Creationism Trumps Evolution," CBS News, November 22, 2004, http://www.cbsnews.com/stories/2004/11/22/opinion/polls/main657083.shtml.

11. Jon Britton, "Richest two percent own half of world's wealth," PSLweb.org, December 15, 2006, http://www.pslweb.org/site/News2?page=NewsArticle&id=6172.

12. Jalal al-Din Rumi, "Breadmaking," *Rumi: The Book of Love: Poems of Ecstasy and Longing,* trans. Coleman Barks (New York: HarperCollins, 2003) 75–76. Reprinted by permission of the translator.

13. Martin Portner, "The Orgasmic Mind: The Neurological Roots of Sexual Pleasure," *Scientific American Mind,* April 2008, http://www.scientificamerican.com/article.cfm?id=the-orgasmic-mind.

14. Kahlil Gibran, "Marriage," *The Prophet,* (1923).

ACKNOWLEDGMENTS

There are many persons who contributed to the creation of this book. First and foremost I would like to express my gratitude to my editors, Patty Gift, Nancy Peske, and Sally Mason, who shaped and sculpted the manuscript into life. I would like to thank Linda Fitch and all the teaching staff at the Four Winds Society for holding the vision of illumination for all of our students and being whole-heartedly dedicated to the Great Initiations. This is our book.

ABOUT THE AUTHOR

Alberto Villoldo, Ph.D., has trained as a psychologist and medical anthropologist, and has studied the healing practices of the Amazon and the Andean shamans for more than 25 years. While at San Francisco State University, he founded the Biological Self-Regulation Laboratory to study how the mind creates psychosomatic health and disease. Dr. Villoldo directs The Four Winds Society, where he trains individuals in the U.S. and Europe in the practice of shamanic healing. He directs the Center for Energy Medicine at Los Lobos, Chile, where he investigates and practices the neuroscience of enlightenment.

Website: **www.thefourwinds.com**

Notes

Notes

Notes

Notes

HAY HOUSE TITLES OF RELATED INTEREST

YOU CAN HEAL YOUR LIFE, the movie,
starring Louise Hay & Friends
(available as a 1-DVD program, an expanded 2-DVD set, and
an online streaming video)
Learn more at www.hayhouse.com/louise-movie

THE SHIFT, the movie,
starring Dr. Wayne W. Dyer
(available as a 1-DVD program, an expanded 2-DVD set, and
an online streaming video)
Learn more at www.hayhouse.com/the-shift-movie

EXCUSES BEGONE!: How to Change Lifelong,
Self-Defeating Thinking Habits,
by Dr. Wayne W. Dyer

THE FUTURE IS NOW: Timely Advice for Creating a Better World,
by His Holiness the 17th Gyalwang Karmapa, Ogyen Trinley Dorje

THE BIOLOGY OF BELIEF: Unleashing the Power
of Consciousness, Matter & Miracles,
by Bruce H. Lipton, Ph.D.

POWER vs. FORCE: The Hidden Determinants of Human Behavior,
by David R. Hawkins, M.D., Ph.D.

THE END OF FEAR: A Spiritual Path for Realists,
by Richard Schaub, Ph.D., with Bonney Gulino Schaub, R.N.

All of the above are available at your local bookstore,
or may be ordered by contacting Hay House (see next page).

We hope you enjoyed this Hay House book. If you'd like to receive our online catalog featuring additional information on Hay House books and products, or if you'd like to find out more about the Hay Foundation, please contact:

Hay House, Inc., P.O. Box 5100, Carlsbad, CA 92018-5100
(760) 431-7695 or (800) 654-5126
(760) 431-6948 (fax) or (800) 650-5115 (fax)
www.hayhouse.com® • www.hayfoundation.org

———

Published in Australia by:
Hay House Australia Pty. Ltd., 18/36 Ralph St., Alexandria NSW 2015
Phone: 612-9669-4299 • *Fax:* 612-9669-4144 • www.hayhouse.com.au

Published in the United Kingdom by:
Hay House UK, Ltd., Astley House, 33 Notting Hill Gate, London W11 3JQ
Phone: 44-20-3675-2450 • *Fax:* 44-20-3675-2451 • www.hayhouse.co.uk

Published in India by: Hay House Publishers India,
Muskaan Complex, Plot No. 3, B-2, Vasant Kunj, New Delhi 110 070
Phone: 91-11-4176-1620 • *Fax:* 91-11-4176-1630 • www.hayhouse.co.in

———

Access New Knowledge.
Anytime. Anywhere.

Learn and evolve at your own pace
with the world's leading experts.

www.hayhouseU.com